Immigrant Learners and Their Families
Literacy to Connect the Generations

Immigrant Learners and Their Families
Literacy to Connect the Generations

Gail Weinstein-Shr & Elizabeth Quintero, Editors

A co-publication of
the Center for Applied Linguistics and Delta Systems Co., Inc.
prepared by the National Clearinghouse for ESL Literacy Education,
an adjunct ERIC Clearinghouse

Language in Education

Theory & Practice

CAL ©1995 by the Center for Applied Linguistics
and by Delta Systems Co., Inc.

Printed in the United States of America

10 9 8 7 6 5 4 3 2 1

Language in Education: Theory and Practice 84

Editorial/production supervision: Joy Peyton and Fran Keenan
Editorial assistance: Amy Fitch
Copyediting: Elizabeth Rangel
Interior design/production: Julie Booth
Cover design/production: Vincent Sagart
Cover illustration: Zola R. Short
ISBN 0-937354-84-8

This publication was prepared with funding from the Office of Educational Research and Improvement, U.S. Department of Education, under contract No. RI 89166001. The opinions expressed in this report do not necessarily reflect the positions or policies of OERI or ED.

Library of Congress Cataloging-in-Publication Data
Immigrant learners and their families: literacy to connect the generations / Gail
Weinstein-Shr and Elizabeth Quintero, editors.
    p. cm. — (Language in education ; 84)
    "Prepared by the National Clearinghouse for ESL Literacy Education."
    Includes bibliographic references.
    ISBN 0-937354-84-8
    1. Immigrants—Education—United States—Case studies. 2. Family literacy pro-
grams—United States—Case studies. I. Weinstein-Shr, Gail. II. Quintero, Eliza-
beth P. III. Center for Applied Linguistics. IV. National Clearinghouse for ESL
Literacy Education. V. Series.
LC3731.I55 1995
371.96'75'0973—dc20   94-19991

CONTENTS

FOREWORD i
Brian V. Street

PREFACE
Gail Weinstein-Shr 1

SECTION I
Program Design: Focus on Collaboration 5

CHAPTER 1
Literacy Program Design: Reflections from California 11
Grace D. Holt and Daniel D. Holt

CHAPTER 2
Lessons in Collaboration: An Adult Educator's Perspective 19
Jessica Dilworth

CHAPTER 3
Connecting Through Culture Brokers: Promise and Pitfalls 33
Nora Lewis and Cecelia Varbero

CHAPTER 4
Family Collaboration in Children's Literacy:
When Journals Travel Home 43
Daniel J. Doorn

SECTION II
Curriculum: Drawing on Learner Strengths   *59*

CHAPTER 5
From Deficit to Strength: Changing Perspectives on Family Literacy   63
Elsa Roberts Auerbach

CHAPTER 6
Memories of Mami in the Family Literary Class   77
Loren McGrail

CHAPTER 7
Literacy from Within: The Project FIEL Curriculum   91
Ana Huerta-Macías

CHAPTER 8
Our Stories to Transform Them: A Source of Authentic Literacy   101
Maritza Arrastía

SECTION III
Where We Are, Where We're Going   *111*

CHAPTER 9
Learning from Uprooted Families   113
Gail Weinstein-Shr

CHAPTER 10
Evidence of Success: Learner Assessment and Program Evaluation in Innovative Programs   135
Heide Spruck Wrigley

CHAPTER 11
Magic and Risk: Lessons for the Future   149
Elizabeth Quintero

AUTHOR BIOGRAPHIES   163

FOREWORD

Brian V. Street
University of Sussex, UK; University of Pennsylvania

Viewing from a distance—as a British social anthropologist and as a literacy researcher—the growth of interest in family literacy in the United States (now being followed by the United Kingdom), there seem to me to have been two basic approaches or philosophies of education involved in the movement. One of these, and the dominant one until recently, has been the cultural deficit model; the other is the culturally sensitive model.

Within the cultural deficit model, educators, politicians, programme directors, and funders have seen the family, and links between generations in the family, as a way of achieving educational goals that schools were unable to achieve. At its most extreme, this involved using family literacy schemes to infuse school and middle-class values and forms of literacy into diverse homes. These homes were seen as in cultural deficit—lacking the qualities of educational support and cognitive skill required of formal schooling, which was taken to be why so many children from them failed in the school system. The solution, then, was to take the school to the home—to teach parents how to be proper teachers of their children such as how to read to them in approved ways and to inculcate the ways of learning, speaking, reading, and writing valued in mainstream education.

This project has all the hallmarks of many Third World literacy programs in which the same assumptions about cultural deficit have been made and in which the assumed superiority of First World societies has led to a missionary spirit for transferring our so-called "advantages" and "truth" to them. In the case of Third World campaigns, the vast failure of most to attract so-called "illiterate" learners to classes or, having persuaded them into classes, to keep them there, or having seen them through several literacy learning thresholds, to help them maintain that literacy in contexts where it was not required, has led to radical rethinking about the nature of literacy itself and of the programmes intended to deliver literacy instruction (see, e.g., Verhoeven, 1994). Similar rethinking has not always been so prominent in industrialised societies as they encounter the growing number of people who have literacy difficulties. Instead, top-down assumptions about delivery and imparting of particular literacy practices to the so-called illiterate, and stereotypes about sad, empty illiterates living in darkness and awaiting the light of middle-class schooled literacy, continue to dominate media representation. The crisis of illiteracy remains rooted in an assumption of a single, homogenous society and a single, homogenous literacy required of its members. As with representations of life in poorer countries, the assumptions about life in non-mainstream America—whether amongst new immigrants, minority groups, or poor sectors of urban society—fail to see the richness, complexity, and diversity of other peoples' lives. Educational programmes, particularly those focussed on literacy, are particularly prone to this myopia, and so instead of building upon what is there already—the complex uses of different literacy practices in everyday life evident now from research on different cultural groups—they continue to purvey a single, narrow definition of literacy and attempt to impose it on their subjects. It could be argued that the single major cause of continuing school failure and literacy difficulties lies in the cultural misunderstandings between those providing literacy instruction and those receiving it.

In recent years, however, recognition of the significance of cultural misunderstanding and the problems it raises has increased, fed partly—as with Third World campaigns—by the continuing failure of mainstream programmes and partly by the increased knowledge through research (whether by academics or by teachers and facilitators themselves) into the lives, cultures, and varied literacy practices of different groups of people. This culturally sensitive model underpins the present volume and points forward, I believe, to a new partnership in education not only across generations but also across cultures and classes. According to this model, people with literacy difficulties in some parts of their lives already have some knowledge of literacy and live in cultural settings where various kinds of literacy are valued. The problem for mainstream teachers is that these forms of knowledge and life are not always apparent. Precisely because they involve cultural beliefs and practices and not just formal technical skills of the kind teachers are used to dealing with in literacy classes, they are not always easily recognised. They might, for instance, as Maritza Arrastía shows in Chapter 8, involve ideas about story and narrative that differ in some ways from mainstream norms; or they might, as Weinstein-Shr shows in Chapter 9, involve cultural assumptions about how knowledge is displayed and where and by whom it is appropriate for certain kinds of speech and literacy to be presented. They may, as Heath (1983) showed in her classic ethnography of literacy that is frequently cited in this volume, involve assumptions about collective rather than individual uses of reading and writing: the kinds of collaboration detailed in Section 1. Once it is recognised that people from non-mainstream backgrounds do not come tabula rasa to the education system—that they come bringing trails of their own cultural heritage and that this is frequently why they have difficulty seeing what the mainstream teacher takes for granted—then whole new possibilities and fields of work and enquiry are opened up. Instead of showing frustration or even scorn at the inability of their students to do things that seem straightforward to them, these culturally sensitive (Villegas, 1991) educators start by building upon what is already there. This involves, as Auerbach stresses in Chapter 5, listening to what their students have to say. It also involves finding out about the lives and cultural meanings of not only the students who come to classes but also of those students' families: their children and grandchildren, their parents and grandparents. This, then, is where family literacy takes on a new and richer dimension than in the dominant culture deficit approach.

The descriptions in this volume of attempts to find out about the diverse cultures and the literacies within the United States are ample testimony themselves to the value of this approach. They detail both the richness and complexity of the lives that lie beneath what teachers often see in classes; the shy student who seldom speaks becomes suddenly transformed into an exciting and excited story teller when given space and legitimacy to describe her own story. But— and this is what is so significant for mainstream teachers and not just for anthropologists like myself already interested in cultural diversity—this work and understanding also energises and excites the teachers. They learn, too, and what they learn evidently makes them better teachers. Although we may already know this in theory—that the best teachers are those who can listen and learn, not just impart what they know to others—what the present volume achieves is a deep and detailed insight into how this works in practice across a range of cultural and linguistic differences. The volume is important, therefore, at a more general level than just—as the title suggests—immigrant families. Important and numerous though this category of people is in present-day America, the findings presented here speak to a broader category—to the society as a whole. For the differences that are apparent here across linguistic and historically different cultural backgrounds of immigrants are also present in perhaps less evident ways in all schooling. Children whose parents and grandparents have lived in America for many generations and no longer are thought of as immigrants—indeed, have no experience of life in other countries—also come to school with their own rich cultural values and literacy practices and are frequently misunderstood. The project suggested here, then, is no less than the transformation of education itself, of which the present volume is but a case study from particular immigrant groups. This transformation must involve the recognition that all learners carry with them cultural assumptions about what they are learning, and about how and what is appropriate in their "ways with words," as Heath (1983) describes. Therefore, teachers must become cultural anthropologists of a kind, alert to signs of difference and to where students are coming from and equally self-conscious about their own cultural assumptions and about how they might be viewed by students.

This self-consciousness, moreover, extends beyond the classroom. The accounts in this volume show, as Weinstein-Shr stresses, the necessity of shifting focus from the classroom to the wider cultural setting. All of the teachers and programme developers described here learned to do this. It was not always easy, and one of the strengths of the book is the honesty and openness with which the authors spell out the difficulties they faced and the mistakes they made. For instance, Project LEIF in Philadelphia, described by Nora Lewis and Cecilia Varbero in Chapter 3, faced considerable political difficulties at a local level that arose from cultural misunderstandings about who could authentically represent a community. The cultural groups from which learners came were not homogenous, and no one person in a group could speak for all its members. This discovery of variation and diversity—where the deficit model sees only a vacuum—is one of the major strengths of the volume and of the approach it represents. A significant finding that recurs in a number of the accounts is that this cultural sensitivity is important not only for the teachers—who often, though not always, come from different cultural and class backgrounds than their students—but also for the students themselves. Just because someone comes from a particular cultural background, there is no reason to assume that they understand and value that culture. Many young people in immigrant families are so concerned with fitting in with their host society—learning American English and the American life style—that they may cut themselves off from their home language and culture. Ironically, it seems, this very focus upon the American way of life may be a source of difficulty in coming to grips with it: By abandoning their home language and culture, they also cut off links with the older generation—links that, by and large, mainstream students can assume. They thereby lose that support, both emotional and educational, that is crucial to their own learning. The projects described here frequently detail how members of the older generation of immigrants come to classes for literacy and for English language in order to be able to communicate with their children. But what this approach to family literacy also shows is that intergenerational links are two-directional. It seems that it is equally important for children to learn how to communicate with their parents, and this involves them learning their parents' language and culture. Sociologists have often described a pattern in which third-generation immigrant children lose touch with their parents' language and culture but then begin to search for their cultural roots and maintain their cultural heritage. The present volume suggests that this process is now being speeded up: First generation children are losing touch with their background but some are already beginning to see the disadvantages of that and are attempting to rebuild their linguistic and cultural knowledge. The programs described here, ranging from language collaboration in British Columbia to bilingual programs in California and a mothers' reading program in New York City, show the ways in which this intergenerational collaboration can be assisted by sensitive educators and the educational as well as cultural gains of doing so.

The papers collected here also represent an important contribution to literacy research more generally—what I have termed the "new literacy studies" (Street, 1994). Whereas previously research into literacy was conducted mainly on an experimental basis, and it was assumed that there was a single *Literacy* to be studied (with a big "L" and a singular "y"), it is now recognized that there are multiple literacies that vary with culture and setting, and so different methods of research are necessary. This has led to use of ethnographic studies based on detailed observation and participation by a researcher over lengths of time, on the model of anthropological research whereby the anthropologist learns the language and the culture of the people he or she is studying by living amongst them often for a number of years. The ethnographies of literacy that emerge from this process have given us deeper insights into literacy practices and a sounder basis for program development as Auerbach argues (in Chapter 5 of this volume). But this has not been the province solely of academic researchers, providing top-down studies that enhance their own career within academic culture. In recent years, the teacher-research movement (highlighted in an important book by Susan Lytle and Marilyn Cochran-Smith, 1993) has demonstrated the value of teachers' own knowledge and insights. The present volume builds on this, in that many of the articles are written by teachers or facilitators describing their own programs and experiences, and also extends it in that some of the accounts are by the program developers, as in the case of Grace and Daniel Holt, who helped design, implement, and evaluate family literacy projects in California. As a result, the accounts have the freshness and involvement of those actually working in the area and the advantage of the kind of "inside knowledge" referred to by Lytle and Cochran-Smith (1993). At the same time, they retain the detachment that has been gained by the academic advances in understanding of multiple literacies and that puts into broader perspective the teacher-researcher-program developer's own literacy and avoids the cultural imperialism of the deficit model.

This, then, is an important book. It is important for researchers in extending our knowledge of family literacy amongst immigrant families and in applying insights from the field of literacy studies to new areas of cultural experience. It is important for educators and practitioners in showing the gains to be made from a culturally sensitive approach and the possibilities for doing their own research. It is important for members of immigrant and minority families in showing how it has been possible to reinforce their cultural heritage in new situations through an intimate linkage with the learning of literacy. And it is important in linking theory and practice in ways that can only be to the advantage of learners and teachers alike.

I hope that it will receive wide attention and will help to connect not only generations but also cultures and classes in the diverse literacy environments we now inhabit.

References

Heath, S. B. (1983). *Ways with words*. Cambridge: Cambridge University Press.

Lytle, S., & Cochran-Smith, S. (Eds.). (1993). *Inside/outside: Teacher research and knowledge*. New York: Columbia University, Teachers' College.

Street, B. (Ed.). (1994). The new literacy studies [Special Issue]. *Journal of Research in Reading, 16*(2).

Verhoeven, L. (Ed.). (1994). *Functional literacy: Theoretical issues and educational implications*. Amsterdam/Philadelphia: John Benjamins.

Villegas, A. M. (1991). *Culturally responsive teaching*. Princeton, NJ: Educational Testing Service.

PREFACE

Gail Weinstein-Shr

My great-grandmother took a boat from Poland to Brooklyn, New York, with her children, one of whom was my grandmother, Nana Re. When my mother and aunt were born, Nana Re wanted them to learn English quickly so that they could succeed in America. Except for a few colorful expressions, my mother and aunt did not learn Yiddish; my great-grandmother never learned English. They lived in the same home, unable to talk with one another. Great-grandmother eventually died, a lonely stranger in the home of her own children and grandchildren. At the age of 60, my aunt still becomes tearful as she tells of her grandmother and as she fathoms her own lost opportunities.

Chet Chia, a young Cambodian poet laments:

Their mothers barely speak English.
One day the child swears at her
    and she says "thank-you."
On that day
    in front of everyone
Friends and relatives
    hear the children curse their mother.
They feel ill at ease.
What kind of woman is she not to be ashamed?
The children have forgotten Khmer
    because their parents are shortsighted.
They're afraid their children won't know
    how to speak English.
They don't worry
    that they've already forgotten Khmer.

(From *Cambodia's Lament: A Selection of Cambodian Poetry*, edited and published by George Chigas, 1991, Millers Falls, MA. Reprinted by permission.)

Can it be that, nearly a century after my great-grandmother arrived in the United States, we have not been able to learn from her grief and the grief of her grandchildren? Can it be that the Cambo-

1

dian children I know will wait, like my aunt, until they are 60 years old and it is too late?

Each of us who teaches English as a second language knows a family or a family member like this. We know adults who feel humiliated as their children take over English-speaking encounters. We hear tales of frustration as parents feel increasingly helpless to discipline their children or to help them in school. We know children who feel embarrassed when their parents cannot do what the parents of American peers do. We know more than one child who has missed school to translate for a relative at a doctor's office. We know children who signal in one hundred ways that they are desperate to have an adult in their lives who is in control. It is clear to me that when a member of any generation is pained in an intergenerational encounter, members of all the generations involved in this encounter must be equally pained.

The seeds for this book were sown when my colleague, D. Scott Enright, wrote to me several years ago to ask about my intergenerational work. In 1985, Nancy Henkin, Director of Temple University's Center for Intergenerational Learning, had invited me to set up a tutoring program for refugees. One of my tasks was to train college students to tutor older learners or elders in English. At Learning English through Intergenerational Friendship, or Project LEIF as it came to be called (see Chapter 3, this volume, for a description of the program), my initial "survival syllabus" didn't work: Elders didn't need to fill out forms. Their children and grandchildren did it for them. They had no interest in supermarket labels; they wanted to eat their own familiar food.

The elders at Project LEIF *did* want their grandchildren to know something about their country of origin. They wanted to tell them about the waterfalls not far from their huts, about water buffalo fights, about their playful and elaborate courting songs, and about how they escaped from their countries using their will and their wits. At Project LEIF, the curriculum has slowly shifted from survival competencies to survival stories. Elders who once had little use for English have found themselves motivated to tell their stories, to read one another's, and to write them down in English for their grandchildren; these stories have become the curriculum. The newsletters that result from collected stories have become reading material for elders to bring home to their families.

As I worked with elders, it became clear that I could not think about the needs of adults without also thinking of children. For elders, one form of survival is cultural transmission: the assurance that one's story will be carried on through future generations. For elders, children *are* survival. It is through children that memory, value, and meaning are embodied and continued. I told Scott about the adults and elders I knew, and of the role of language in connecting elders, or impeding connection, to their children and grandchildren.

Scott told me of his own work with children, and his passionate belief that children are best equipped to manage against the odds when they can draw strength from parents, grandparents, and their own past. It was in these early conversations that I began to ponder the promise of collaboration between child and adult educators. As I continue to talk to my colleagues in child education, I am also becoming convinced that part of survival for children is to know who they are and where they have come from. It is because of this belief that I find literacy such a potentially powerful tool for connecting generations, to help adults interact joyfully with their children, and to help children find ways to connect to the worlds of experience that their elders have brought from another place and another time.

I am pleased that Elizabeth Quintero, an authority on early childhood education, has joined me in inviting you to read the work of others, work we believe provides examples from which to learn. We invite you to struggle with us in examining our own work and in striving to be sure that our efforts with uprooted children and adults may serve to heal rather than divide the generations and the cultures.

I

Program Design: Focus on Collaboration

The terms *family literacy* and *intergenerational literacy* have recently gained attention as a growing body of research confirms the importance of social context in the development of various literacies. Although these terms have different meanings to different people, most who use them agree that the relationships between children and adults are important, and that these relationships profoundly affect the meaning of literacy as well as the development of specific literacy skills and practices.

Family and intergenerational literacy programs may have a wide range of goals. One set of goals that has been most dominant in the field revolves around supporting parents in promoting the school success of their children. To this end, a number of family literacy program initiatives have emerged, such as the Barbara Bush Family Literacy Foundation, the Even Start legislation, and the Family English Literacy Program of the Office of Bilingual Education and Minority Languages Affairs (OBEMLA). In these initiatives, one stated purpose is to assist parents who desire more educational skills for themselves, so they can make sure that their children reach their full potential as learners. Central to this agenda is a focus on increased parental involvement in their children's schooling. Programs aimed at increasing parental involvement in schooling use activities that encourage or teach parents to do the following:

1. Provide a home environment that supports children's learning needs;

2. Volunteer in the schools as aides or in other roles;

Some of the material in this introduction appears in Weinstein-Shr (1992), *Family and Intergenerational Literacy in Multilingual Families*, available free from the National Clearinghouse for ESL Literacy Education, Center for Applied Linguistics, Washington, DC.

3. Monitor children's progress and communicate with school personnel; and

4. Tutor children at home to reinforce work done in school (Simich-Dudgeon, 1986).

A second set of goals in family literacy programs has been to "improve skills, attitudes, values, and behaviors linked to reading" (Nickse, 1990, p. 5). Program models that embrace these goals use a variety of reading activities. Those based on work with native English speakers often involve teaching parents to imitate behaviors that occur in the homes of children who are successful in school, such as reading aloud to children or asking children specific types of questions as parents read. Parents of young children may practice in adult groups using books that they then read to their children.

As we learn more about the lives of learners in multilingual communities, it becomes apparent that some of the goals and techniques traditionally used in family literacy programs, though appropriate in certain settings, may be problematic with some multilingual families. An emphasis on nuclear families, for example, may miss the realities of households that have been reconstituted in flight from countries of origin. As we examine the roles of languages and literacies in the lives of those we seek to serve, it becomes impossible to overlook the obstacles faced by multilingual families where adults are rarely in a position to master more English than their children, to be able to help with school work, or to read stories to their children in a language that is not their own. These realities present us with the challenge of envisioning broader goals and developing creative new approaches to our intergenerational work. The accounts in these pages document some of the attempts to grapple with these issues.

A third set of goals, then, is to "increase the social significance of literacy in family life by incorporating community cultural forms and social issues into the content of literacy activities" (Auerbach, 1990, p. 17). With these goals, program activities address family and community concerns, attend to the role of home language and culture, and include activities to enable adults to develop a critical understanding of schooling to evaluate and rehearse appropriate responses while developing networks for individual or group advocacy (Auerbach, this volume). This model challenges the assumption that it is the job of the parents alone to accommodate schools; rather, schools and community members are seen to have equal responsibility for understanding and accommodating one another's agendas.

Finally, some programs have grown out of the unique difficulties experienced by immigrant families, including stresses exacerbated by the differences in the pace of language acquisition for the different generations. Children who have more exposure to English are often placed in a position of translating and solving other problems for parents, reversing traditional roles and creating stress for youth and adults (Weinstein-Shr & Henkin, 1991). Involuntary displacement, and in extreme cases, cultural genocide (such as among Cambodians) may severely interrupt natural processes of cultural transmission. In programs such as Project LEIF, Learning English through Intergenerational Friendship (see Chapter 3, this volume), or the Mothers' Reading Program (see Chapter 8, this volume), one of the goals is to reestablish channels for cultural transmission between the generations through oral history and storytelling.

Tapping cultural riches while addressing the needs of multilingual families cannot be done by any one group or organization singlehandedly. The work of forging relationships between schools and communities, of bridging cultures and healing generations, requires partnership from each side of these divides. In Atlanta, Georgia, child and adult educators found that their differences in training and teaching philosophies had to be negotiated in Project CLASS, which held adult classes, child classes, and jointly designed intergenerational activities (Nurss & Rawlston, 1992). Ironically, through the struggles and conversations around the task of designing joint activities, both sets of teachers ended up reflecting on practice in ways that changed their own teaching practices in traditional one-generation classrooms. In the Nobody's Perfect Project in Vancouver, British Columbia (Ritch, 1992), community workers and ESL curriculum designers had to learn to "talk each other's language" as they collaborated to create parent groups that addressed language learning and parenting issues simultaneously. Whereas agendas may not be the same, by understanding the diversity and negotiating common ground, all players can be strengthened, and our work can take on a new and stronger life of its own. It is for this reason that we have chosen to focus our selections for Part I, Program Design, on the theme of collaboration.

In "Literacy Program Design: Reflections from California," Grace and Daniel Holt reflect on their years of experience with the California Office of Bilingual Education, in which they supported and oversaw federally funded family literacy projects. Their work with educators throughout California makes evident their commitment to the bilingual family as an interdependent unit that can be strengthened through our efforts as educators. In their chapter, Holt and Holt describe some of the forms that projects may take. It is clear from their work that program design, though based on certain principles of sound educational practice, may be as diverse as the communities that are being served.

Although the notion of collaboration is frequently advocated, in "Lessons in Collaboration: An Adult Educator's Perspective," Jessica Dilworth describes her experience at Sunnyside UP in Tuscon, Arizona, to show us that in the world of real people, collaboration is not easy. As through "the layers of an onion skin," Dilworth leads us on a tour of the struggles encountered at every level as different agencies, adult and child educators, and program participants negotiate their ways of working with each other. In Sunnyside UP, as in programs everywhere, participants and program staff necessarily pursue their own agendas, which may or may not be explicit at first. The payoff comes as partners begin to understand and articulate both their own and one another's agendas. This makes it possible to deal effectively with conflicts and to come up with ways of cooperating that meet each participant's needs. Dilworth's description illustrates that the cost in time, energy, and hard work pays off richly in a program that is stronger than the sum of its parts.

Yet another kind of collaboration occurs when members of ethnic communities provide links between their compatriots and educational organizations that wish to serve them. In "Connecting Through Culture Brokers: Promise and Pitfalls," Nora Lewis and Cecelia Varbero reflect on their experiences coordinating Project LEIF in Philadelphia, Pennsylvania. Specifically, they examine the role of bilingual assistants and community leaders, key players who have linked LEIF with the Hmong, Cambodian, Chinese, and Hispanic communities over the years. Their chapter indicates the danger of making assumptions about people based on their ethnicity or about communities as monolithic entities. It is clear that in order to serve any community effectively, it is necessary to take an inquiring stance toward the structure of the community and the role of each member within it. It is only in this way that we can develop appropriate expectations of our bilingual and bicultural colleagues. Better knowledge about the communities we seek to serve may also help us to understand the inevitable silences that sometimes meet the heartfelt invitations to our programs that we extend to our ethnically different neighbors.

Finally, in "Family Collaboration in Children's Literacy: When Journals Travel Home," Dan Doorn shows the possibilities for collaboration among children themselves in their own classrooms, as well as between children and their caregivers. Doorn's work, like Dilworth's, shows that partnership does not happen overnight. It is nurtured in small, trust-building steps. This chapter also shows that collaboration need not be a mysterious process shrouded in high-level committee meetings; rather, it can be part of the very fabric of our way of teaching in every child or adult classroom. Doorn's work teaches us, through his wonderful tales of children's writing, that education is an infinitely hopeful endeavor, and that we have the power to facilitate discovery while children and adults, natives and newcomers, draw strength and sustenance from our newly developing multicultural and intergenerational communities.

References

Auerbach, E.R. (1990). *Making meaning, making change: A guide to participatory curriculum development for adult ESL and family literacy.* Boston: University of Massachusetts, Boston Family Literacy Project. (Revised and published as Auerbach, E.R., 1992, *Making meaning, making change: Participatory curriculum development for adult ESL literacy.* Washington, DC and McHenry, IL: Center for Applied Linguistics and Delta Systems Co.)

Nickse, R. (1990). Foreword. In M. McIvor (Ed.), *Family literacy in action: A survey of successful programs.* Syracuse, NY: New Readers Press.

Nurss, J., & Rawlston, S. (1992). *Project CLASS: Collaboration among ages and agencies.* Unpublished manuscript.

Ritch, A. (1992). *Nobody's perfect/ESL: A collaborative process.* Unpublished manuscript.

Simich-Dudgeon, C. (1986). *Parent involvement and the education of limited-English-proficient students.* Washington, DC: Center for Applied Linguistics. (ERIC Document Reproduction Service No. ED 279 205)

Weinstein-Shr, G. (1992). *Family and intergenerational literacy in multilingual families. ERIC Q&A.* Washington, DC: Center for Applied Linguistics, National Clearinghouse on Literacy Education. (ERIC Document Reproduction Service No. ED 321 624)

Weinstein-Shr, G., & Henkin, N. (1991). Continuity and change: Intergenerational relations in Southeast Asian refugee families. *Marriage and Family Review, 16*(3), 351-367.

CHAPTER 1

Literacy Program Design: Reflections from California

Grace D. Holt and Daniel D. Holt

Most of the efforts in California directed at promoting literacy for language minority adults take place in Family English Literacy Programs (FELP) implemented under Title VII of the Elementary and Secondary Education Act (ESEA). Since 1986, we have worked with staff in approximately 36 of these projects to plan, implement, and evaluate them. In these projects, the term *family English literacy* is used to describe an instructional design that includes English language development for the parents and literacy activities designed to strengthen parent-child communication and the children's overall school achievement. This chapter provides an overview of the projects that have been implemented in California for language minority parents and their children. Although we primarily focus on projects that are consistent with the FELP guidelines contained in ESEA, Title VII, the program features presented here share many of the characteristics of other literacy projects that have the goal of strengthening literacy through the family.

Distinguishing Features of Family Literacy Projects

Several features distinguish FELP projects from other approaches to adult literacy. These features result in part from the view that parents are the most important teachers of their children and that literacy is fostered most effectively when it is promoted within the family as well as the school. The distinguishing features of FELP projects in California are summarized in this section.

First, we have learned that it is critical to assess the needs of project participants. The purpose of a comprehensive needs assessment is to identify learners' strengths and provide curriculum content that is useful and meaningful. Although a variety of approaches are used to determine learners' strengths and needs, we have found that a needs assessment is most successful when designed and implemented through direct, face-to-face interaction with the participants.

Needs assessments have enabled us to design appropriate curriculum content, class schedules, and class locations. For example, staff in one project were able to ascertain that the most appropriate site for classes was in one of the units in an apartment complex that housed a large number of recent immigrants. In another project, the needs assessment indicated that parents would be more willing to attend classes if child care and transportation were provided (Holt, 1994).

Second, we have come to recognize that effective literacy projects have multiple outcomes. While promoting literacy development, it is imperative to address other issues that participants identify as important as well. For example, in one project, parents who were concerned about two deaths from drowning asked FELP staff for information about helping their children learn to swim. The staff worked with a local community organization to arrange swimming lessons for families. FELP classes focused on life saving and first-aid information and the language strategies needed to talk about swimming safety. Thus, literacy development was fostered through a focus on a nonlinguistic problem.

Third, FELP projects in California aim to implement on-site activities in which parents and their children learn and work together. In some projects, such activities have been quite successful. However, in others, parents have expressed ambivalent, sometimes negative attitudes toward bringing their children to class. We have had to adjust each project to respond to parents' wishes about the structure of the classes and the degree to which children are directly involved in the program design. In projects where children and parents participate together, we have found that staff need to be familiar with effective approaches for dealing with both older and younger learners.

Next, we are committed to the benefits of bilingual instruction. Most of our projects in California have staff who are able to provide instruction in English and the learners' native languages. We use the participants' native languages as a medium of instruction for addressing content related to parenting or life skills. In some cases, we help adult learners develop their language and literacy abilities in their native language. We have learned that bilingual approaches allow project staff to increase the comprehensibility of instruction and to convey to the participants our belief that their native languages represent valid and useful resources (*Bilingual Education Handbook*, 1990).

Finally, California FELP projects take place in a variety of settings—in schools attended by the participants' children, in community centers, in the learners' homes, or in a combination of the three. The most important consideration in selecting the project site is to make sure that it is accessible to the participants. Creating easy access to instructional activities helps overcome irregular attendance and attrition, key obstacles to program success.

Family Literacy Program Designs in California

All of our FELP projects share the goal of enhancing the literacy development of nonnative-English-speaking parents and their children. A variety of program designs achieve this goal, depending on the participants' needs, the language and age groups served, the geographic location of the project, and the type of educational or community-based organization administering the project.

Projects evolve as ongoing adjustments are made. Adjustments can involve subtle refinements or dramatic changes depending on the expressed needs of the learners and the staff's knowledge of the learners and their families. This section describes the program types in place in California. A single program type does not correspond to any one project; rather, we have combined the effective features of many projects to come up with three program types, according to the context in which they are found: schools, communities, and homes (*Proceedings from the Family English Literacy Seminar*, 1991).

School-based programs

There are two types of school-based programs—parent-focused, in which the parents' curriculum is coordinated with their children's school activities, and learner-focused, in which parents and staff members collaborate to address topics they have identified as important for literacy development.

Parent-focused programs

In many of our projects, classes are held in an elementary or secondary school attended by the participants' children. Staff work with the participants' children during the day, use bilingual instructional approaches, integrate literacy and parenting instruction, and use curriculum materials written in English and the participants' native language(s). Parents consistently report satisfaction with having classes at their children's school. They enjoy being able to walk to classes and become familiar with the staff, facilities, and general school environment. In many communities, the school represents the only place where parents can gather to share their experiences and discuss their problems. In these school-based programs, we have seen parents' participation in school activities increase as they become more comfortable and knowledgeable about their children's educational experiences.

We have worked with two basic instructional designs in parent-focused programs. The first coordinates parenting skills instruction with literacy development. The second is an intergenerational approach that uses children's literature to develop the literacy skills of parents and children. In projects that focus on parenting skills, we use topics selected by the parents, such as education, safety, and nutrition. Instruction is delivered in both English and the native language. For example, while the parents are working on literacy activities that will help them register their children in school, they may have a group discussion in their native language in which they compare and contrast discipline techniques they use at home with those used by teachers at school (Holt, 1988). One bilingual instructor teaches in both languages, or one monolingual instructor team teaches with a bilingual facilitator. In either case, we have realized the importance of having staff who are well trained to deliver instruction in both English and the native language of the learners and of coordinating literacy instruction with content requested by the learners.

In programs focusing on an intergenerational approach, children participate with their parents in literacy activities either in the classroom or at home, in an attempt to promote parent-child interaction and strengthen the parent-child relationship. These activities are more successful with parents who have developed some basic literacy skills in their native language or in English than with nonliterate parents, who are often more interested in developing literacy skills they can use immediately to address their own survival needs.

In intergenerational programs, we employ selections from the children's language arts program as content for the parents' literacy instruction. State-approved reading lists are used to select reading material for each grade level. Often, parents are grouped based on their literacy levels and the grade level of their children. The most effective instructors are those who are bilingual in English and the native language of the participants and are well versed in techniques that use books to promote interaction between parents and children.

The intergenerational approach is tailored to the parents' literacy level. If parents have limited literacy skills, we provide instruction in the native language and describe strategies for using books with cassette tapes, using pictures to tell stories, or having children read aloud. Parents who have developed literacy skills in English commensurate with their children's grade levels may choose to read books to their children in English and ask questions and discuss the books in English or in their native languages. Parent-child activities may take place in the classroom where the staff members can observe and give feedback to the parents, or they may be conducted at home with follow-up discussions in the class.

Learner-focused programs

In this approach, staff collaborate with parents to develop the content of instruction based on the parents' needs, not necessarily tied to those of their children. The content of the curriculum is determined by the learners and staff members working together, and we encourage parent learners to assist in monitoring and evaluating the project activities on an ongoing basis. We have developed and refined this model using the process described below:

1. Staff and learners collaborate to implement activities such as individual interviews and focus groups to identify themes that the learners consider important (for example, the family, the community, or the school) and that become the basis for the curriculum content.

2. Activities such as language experience stories are conducted to develop the learners' literacy as they examine each theme.

3. Learners are encouraged to consider their literacy needs outside the classroom, in their communities, work places, and other contexts.

4. Learners evaluate their own progress as well as other aspects of the project. Ongoing evaluation helps staff and learners make necessary adjustments to the overall program design. Because instructional activities are dependent on learners' input, at least one staff member who is proficient in the learners' native language(s) is needed to elicit and respond to their suggestions.

We have learned that the process for developing and implementing the curriculum according to this approach is cyclical. As the program is evaluated and learners identify new themes or ask for different activities to examine the themes, changes are made to the program. Evaluation is used as a continuing process to collect meaningful information that helps improve the program (Holt, 1994).

Community-based programs

Community-based programs in California feature a literacy and parenting design that is similar to the school-based programs; the location of classes is their unique feature. In such programs, fixed or mobile community education centers make the literacy classes more accessible to the participants. Some projects use converted units in apartment complexes where many of the participants live. The units remain open throughout the day and become hubs for classes as well as numerous related program services, including tutoring and counseling services for parents and children. The center is also convenient for people who cannot regularly attend classes. Staff members in the center are able to maintain close contact with community residents, even if they do not attend classes, and in some projects, some staff members actually live in the complex where the center is located. Our experience indicates that having the staff in the midst of the participants' communities provides many opportunities to develop supportive relationships between staff and learners.

Another way we have provided access to literacy programs is through a mobile community center. Some projects have converted a vehicle such as a school bus or bookmobile into a mobile classroom. In one project, the mobile unit was particularly effective in providing services to agricultural workers, whose long and irregular working hours made it difficult for them to attend regular classes. The mobile center was maintained by the school district, and instruction included activities designed to promote literacy through topics that the parents identified as important. Staff were bilingual and were members of the communities served by the project.

Home-based programs

Some FELP projects include activities conducted in participants' homes. Home-based programs may take two forms: a home-school program, in which classroom instruction is followed by activities at home, and a home-tutoring program, in which instruction is conducted exclusively in the home.

In home-school programs, in addition to working on literacy development at a designated school site, participants learn about educational activities they can conduct at home with their children. After the home activity is completed, the participants discuss their experiences in class. One example of a home learning activity used in our projects is shared reading and writing. Parents and children collaborate to write and illustrate language experience stories or family histories in English or in the native language of the participants (Holt & Gaer, 1993). Parents and children work together to bind the stories into books, which are kept in the class library for other participants to read. In some projects, the staff make multiple copies to distribute to the children's classrooms and school libraries.

In home-tutoring programs, staff members travel to participants' homes to tutor individuals or small groups in literacy-related activities. Staff members who observe family members working together in their home environment can help parents and children design literacy events that are compatible with their own needs and experiences. Our experience has shown that the success of this type of program depends largely on a trusting relationship between staff and learners. It is important for staff members to have the cultural knowledge required to be welcome in participants' homes and to be resourceful in developing literacy activities. Learners often report that they are most comfortable with visits by staff who live in their communities and know their culture and language.

In many FELP projects, staff members hold meetings for parents at their children's schools to present the purpose of the program before actual tutoring sessions begin. Meetings are often arranged as social events to reduce the anxiety that parents may feel about school meetings and home visits. After discussing the purpose of the program, staff and parents schedule the home tutoring sessions. In some of our projects, families that are uncomfortable with staff visits to their homes have chosen to meet staff members at an alternative location. In other projects, participants who live near each other have opted to meet in small groups with staff and take turns hosting the sessions.

Conclusion

In this chapter we have described the types of family literacy programs that have been tried in California and offered insights we have gained from the staff and learners associated with specific FELP projects. We have organized the program types as composites of successful approaches to literacy development for language minority families. They exist as alternatives for staff and learners to consider as they design projects that are appropriate for their own needs in specific contexts.

References

Bilingual education handbook: Designing instruction for LEP students. (1990). Sacramento, CA: California Department of Education, Bilingual Education Office. (ERIC Document Reproduction Service No. ED 326 049)

Holt, D. (Ed.). (1994). *Assessing success in family literacy projects: Alternative approaches to assessment and evaluation.* Washington, DC and McHenry, IL: Center for Applied Linguistics and Delta Systems.

Holt, G. (1988). *Parenting curriculum for language minority parents.* Sacramento, CA: California State University, Cross Cultural Resource Center. (ERIC Document Reproduction Service No. ED 318 281)

Holt, G., & Gaer, S. (1993). *Bridge to literacy: English for success.* San Diego: Dominie.

Proceedings from the Family English Literacy Seminar. (1991). Sacramento, CA: California Department of Education, Bilingual Education Office.

CHAPTER 2

Lessons in Collaboration: An Adult Educator's Perspective

Jessica Dilworth

Collaboration is not easy, especially in the early stages of a project when relationships are developing among individuals and institutions. Successful collaboration is determined to a great extent by the strategies we employ to broaden our points of view, to understand our partners, and to alter our usual ways of doing things.

In this chapter, I document my experiences as Family Literacy Coordinator during the first year of a three-year collaborative (called Sunnyside UP) formed by three community-based education providers, each with a track record of success and a history of doing things its own way. This partnership entailed collaborative work among 20 teaching staff, all loyal to their own programs, who initially appeared to have more differences than similarities in their backgrounds, job experiences, and views on education.

Although each of the partners in our collaboration believed in the concept of family literacy and had dabbled in programs in which parents and children learn together, none had really undertaken a family literacy program as comprehensive and intensive as the one we decided to start together. None of us knew just how much understanding and compromise it would take to see the project through its first year.

Formation of Sunnyside UP

In the spring of 1991, five U.S. cities were each awarded a three-year grant from the Toyota Motor Corporation and the National Center for Family Literacy (NCFL) to form collaboratives and implement family literacy programs, combining adult and preschool education in three elementary public school sites. Three educational institutions in Tucson, Arizona, including an adult education agency, a public school system, and a Head Start project, formed a collaborative entity and received one of these grants. Our program is called Sunnyside United with Parents, or Sunnyside UP.

Like the layers of an onion, there are many layers to this collaboration, from funders to clients, as shown in Figure 1. As each layer is peeled off, a complete sphere of its own, another layer can be found, just as complex and vital as the last, functioning independently and interdependently with the other layers. Sunnyside UP consists of seven layers of collaborators.

Funders

At the outer layer is the business and foundation community providing funding: the Toyota Motor Corporation and the Tucson Community Foundation.

The National Center for Family Literacy

At the next layer, NCFL collaborates with states and cities to implement the Kenan Model of family literacy, a model developed at their Kentucky center.

Local partners

Local community agencies pool funds, personnel, and space to create a common vision of education for families.

Public schools

The public school, its staff, and its neighborhood collaborate with preschool and adult education agencies, broadening its definition of what education services it can provide to a community.

Site staff

Site staff (in our case a team of four at each site) learn to work together and integrate early childhood and adult education, in an elementary school setting.

Students and teachers

Staff collaborate with students, both parents and children.

Family members

The deepest layer consists of the families learning what it means for parents and siblings to attend school together in a program with a stated goal of changing family dynamics through a commitment to education.

Figure 1. Multiple layers of involvement in the Sunnyside UP family literacy program

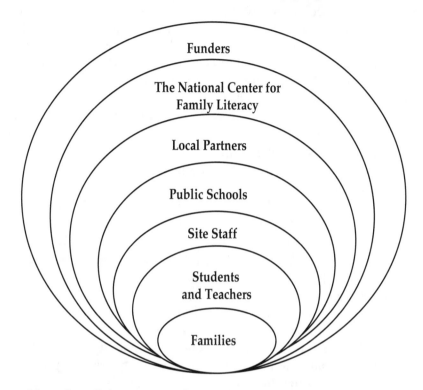

Funders

The National Center for Family Literacy

Local Partners

Public Schools

Site Staff

Students and Teachers

Families

Although collaboration within each layer and between layers has been essential for the program to thrive, the discussion in this chapter focuses on two collaborators in particular: the local partners and the site staff. At Sunnyside UP, there are three local partners:

1. Sunnyside School District
2. Child-Parent Centers, Inc. (CPCI)
3. Pima County Adult Education (where I teach)

Sunnyside School District serves 13,000 students in 17 schools, with a 75% Hispanic and Native American student population. The school district contributes one staff person to each Sunnyside UP project site. That person is a community assistant whose job is to act as a liaison with the public school, to coordinate a parent volunteer program in the school, and to team-teach parent time discussions with the other site staff.

Child-Parent Centers, Inc. (CPCI) is the local recipient of Head Start funding. It serves approximately 1,000 families each year at 23 centers in five counties. (Within the next few years, this number will nearly double due to the expected increase in national funding for Head Start programs.) CPCI offers both classroom and home-based instruction. Parents volunteer in their children's classrooms, and most site staff are neighborhood parents. Parents are also members of CPCI's policy council, which sets direction for Head Start locally. CPCI contributes two early childhood educators to each Sunnyside UP site.

Pima County Adult Education (PCAE) provides adult education services to approximately 10,000 adults a year, age 16 and older. It is an umbrella agency that receives a state grant for adult education as well as grants from federal, state, and local sources. PCAE contributes one adult educator to each Sunnyside UP site and a half-time program coordinator to the project.

Through the collective effort of these three partners, Sunnyside UP serves 15-20 families a year at each of three elementary school sites in a single school district. Each site has two classrooms, one for parents and one for children. Classrooms are run by site staff from the various partner agencies, which include four teachers, two early childhood educators, one public school community assistant, and one adult educator. It has been necessary to work together as a team to create a coherent program that uses the best of our respective expertise to benefit participating families.

To register in the program, a family must live in the school district, meet Head Start income guidelines, enroll a child who is either three or four years of age, and enroll at least one adult with an educational need such as English to Speakers of Other Languages (ESOL); General Educational Development (GED); computer basics; or enrichment in the areas of reading, writing, math, or science. The adults and children attend their neighborhood elementary school from 8:30 a.m. to 3:00 p.m. three days a week.

Adult education classes. We offer ESOL, Adult Basic Education (ABE), and GED preparation, as well as skills enhancement for those parents who have graduated from high school but need to upgrade their basic skills or want to learn to use computers. Some of the parent classes have all ESOL students, but most have a combination of ESOL and GED students.

Early childhood classes. Instructors use the High/Scope curriculum, a language-based, developmental curriculum that encourages child development in decision making.

Parents and Children Together Time (PACT). Parents and children are involved in child-directed activities, parent-initiated learning extensions, and group activities in the children's classroom for 45 minutes every day.

Parent Time discussion (PT). Time is set aside each day for parents to act as a support group for one another. We bring in speakers from the community on topics parents have decided on. We study early childhood development and debrief parents on their interactions with their children during PACT.

Parent volunteer time. Parents volunteer in the public school so they can become part of the school community. They volunteer with teachers, nurses, librarians, and secretaries, or they assist the principal.

Successful Strategies

During the first year of the project, we developed three strategies that helped us keep our collaborative effort together and create a successful program:

1. Allow the staff to create a new program;

2. Focus on developing positive staff relations; and

3. Seek to understand the differences and similarities among the partner agencies.

Strategy I: Allow staff to create a new program

A common problem in beginning a collaboration is that the partners tend to run parallel programs at a common site, rather than creating a new program that offers more than what the individual agencies can offer separately. In Sunnyside UP, all three partners knew they had strengths to contribute from their individual programs and were afraid to make changes that might compromise those strengths. There was not a public statement from all staff that together they were creating something totally different, not just running three successful programs simultaneously using clientele from the same families. Additionally, there was no indication from coordinating staff that teachers could relax their old patterns and create new ones.

The three agencies initially worked separately toward the same goals. The first meeting of the site staff of Sunnyside UP was during a week of implementation training at NCFL headquarters in Louisville, Kentucky, in July. Staff did not really start working in teams during this time because of the rigorous training schedule and the uncertainties of our new roles with one another. When we returned to Tucson, we began synthesizing what our individual programs had to offer, what was written in our grant, and what we had learned in training. We held planning meetings on four levels.

1. *Site staff* met to organize home visits, set up classrooms, and work out details such as scheduling and individual job responsibilities.

2. *Early childhood staff and adult education staff* met separately to discuss the curriculum implications of family literacy.

3. *Full staff* met to understand research and assessment requirements and to discuss concerns about recruitment, child care, attendance, PACT, PT discussions, and vocational components.

4. *Co-directors* met to coordinate food services, start-up details, and a press conference. Principals of participating schools were brought in to meet staff and welcome them to their sites.

It wasn't until several months after the family literacy program was in place that we held a training session in which staff from each collaborating agency presented workshops to the others in the backgrounds, goals, educational philosophies, and classroom approaches of their respective agencies. This was the first formalized step we took to help staff see similarities and differences among our agencies, with the goal of developing more supportive teaching teams. This training was especially helpful for adult educators who had not accurately understood the early childhood curriculum. In observing the structure of the early childhood classroom and the site-to-site standardization of the program, the adult educators assumed the approach of the early childhood educators was prescriptive and at odds with the more liberal principles of adult education. During the training, adult education staff learned than an emergent curriculum in early childhood is synonymous with many aspects of a participatory curriculum in adult education. Both programs emphasize student decision making and train teachers to follow their students. In fact, they have more similarities than differences. For many of us, this was the beginning of a newfound ability to work together and integrate adult and childhood education into the program.

Acknowledging that collaboration can result in the creation of an entirely new program leaves room for staff to learn new ways of doing things. In the beginning of the program, early childhood staff felt they already knew what the parent component would entail, because CPCI had successfully involved parents in its Head Start program before Sunnyside UP. As it turned out, however, adding an adult education focus to their early childhood program brought a lot of frustration; there were more problems when parents and children had to separate into their respective classrooms, more parental scrutiny of the early childhood curriculum, and more parent ideas, issues, and visions to be incorporated into the program than CPCI staff had seen in prior years. It required greater flexibility and changes for early childhood staff to accept parents into their program than for adult education staff to accept children into theirs.

Adding children to the adult education program brought an element of restriction, but mostly added an atmosphere of fun and joy. However, it took about six months for adult education staff to understand the major role and potential of integrating early childhood development into the adult education curriculum. At the beginning of the program, attempts at integrating early childhood and adult education curricula seemed contrived and unnatural; making every GED and ESOL lesson relevant to children, families, and managing a household was uncomfortable. Further, adult educators resisted a team approach to designing the parent curriculum, feeling more comfortable incorporating adult students' needs and interests into class than drawing from the children's or early childhood educators' perspectives. Now, in subsequent years, integration of PT, PACT, early childhood, and adult education lessons into an overall approach is becoming second nature to site staff, improving the quality and effectiveness of our program. Now, topics for most ESOL lessons are derived from what's happening in other components of the program, and parents are more in touch with the early childhood classroom and teachers, as well as with their children's ongoing development. Signs of integration of the components of the program are an indicator that a new program is being created.

To help site staff create a new family literacy program, directors and coordinators must set the tone by deciding which policies, paperwork, and other requirements from their respective agencies can be combined with the new partners, and which can be eliminated. In the first year of Sunnyside UP, early childhood staff had to maintain all the records, policies, events, and activities from the regular Head Start program in addition to implementing new procedures, paperwork, assessments, and activities for Sunnyside UP. This gave them more work and made adapting to the differences of a family literacy program difficult. Early childhood staff were never sure which new ideas they could experiment with and which decisions they could make with their new team without consulting CPCI coordinating staff. Often, staff and parent suggestions were not implemented because early childhood staff had not been given the freedom necessary to make many program decisions in their teams. In the beginning of a new program, each agency should spend time discussing how their new collaboration will be different and how much latitude staff have to respond to new ideas.

Halfway through the first year, early childhood staff thought the children learned more and developed more quickly in the regular Head Start programs than in the family literacy program. Much of this was because these teachers were using the same criteria for evaluating the children's successes that they had used in their previous experiences. We found that children learn rules, develop socially, and adapt to school differently in programs when they are with their parents than when they are on their own. Likewise, adult education staff were frustrated with the parents' progress in GED and ESOL classes because, although the parents were in school for a full day, only a few hours were dedicated to the adult education component. Setting new goals to evaluate progress and effectiveness that fit the new program helped staff make decisions and gauge success more realistically. Now in our second year, we are able to help parents be more realistic about what they can accomplish in one year in the program, and we are able to see ways in which children's attendance at school with their parents affects them more deeply than a Head Start experience where parents are less involved.

Strategy II: Focus on developing positive staff relations

Looking back, I am able to see that some opportunities for integrating the three collaborating programs into one and building personal trust among staff were missed. We focused more attention on the families and the curriculum than on the development of a cohesive staff. We were more worried about teaching the parents techniques in group dynamics than in practicing the techniques among ourselves. Beginnings should be a time for integrating programs and individuals, establishing relationships, developing positive communication patterns, and laying groundwork for understanding the differences and similarities among partnership agencies and individuals. Toward the end of the first year, we started involving staff in workshops including assertiveness training, personality typing, leadership development, and team building. At the end of the first year, staff spent a week debriefing and compiling photo journals documenting the program at each site. The process of creating a product together helped staff find new ways of working as a team. It also focused staff on the accomplishments of the first year and helped them update program and individual goals for the next year. These activities were important steps in building positive staff relations.

As we learn to trust one another and work together, staff will be able to use different criteria for programming, making decisions, and solving problems than we have used in our separate agencies. For example, one component of Sunnyside UP for which staff from all three partners are responsible is Parent Time discussion (PT). In developing curriculum for PT, most early childhood staff wanted to follow a CPCI booklet of lessons designed to help parents learn about issues in early childhood development, which they had previously used in monthly parent meetings at Head Start sites. The adult education staff did not readily accept such a structured curriculum. Pima County Adult Education (PCAE) teachers are trained to develop curriculum jointly with adult students, and to be flexible above all else. We thought the PT curriculum should be based on a participatory approach in which the parents would be actively involved in defining issues, finding multiple solutions, and teaching one another. The two approaches seemed mutually exclusive, and a compromise was not easy to see. After several discussions, we stopped talking about PT as a full staff and allowed it to unfold differently at each of the three sites. By the end of the year, most staff no longer felt that a policy or curriculum for PT had to be agreed on by the full staff. In hindsight, this was actually the best solution. The students and staff at each site need the freedom to develop a PT sequence to fit their circumstances. In the future, developing positive staff relationships before issues like these arise will minimize the potential for divisiveness among staff when solutions to problems are being sought.

Having parents raise issues in PT led first to a problem and then to a compromise that benefited both staff and parents. During the year, parents brought up many issues that were unexpected and unfamiliar to the staff. Adult educators are used to not having all the answers in class and commonly say to their students, "I don't know. Does anyone else have an idea about that? Let's all get some more information." This was a new role for the early childhood educators, who often felt they were put on the spot by the parents' questions and issues.

One site dealt with this by implementing a PT Topics Form that parents could fill out before PT if they had an issue they wanted to talk about. The site team had the chance to look through and think about the parent issues before they came up in a group setting. This made staff appear more unified as a team while also helping parents feel more comfortable in openly expressing their ideas. The added benefit for parents was that they learned to think through their ideas before speaking and to formulate them into writing. By giving priority to developing their working relationships, it became possible for staff to work creatively as a team as unique challenges arose at specific sites.

Strategy III: Seek to understand differences and similarities among partner agencies

Many of the conflicts staff encountered at the site level reflected the different cultures of our respective agencies. In many ways, the ages of our students have dictated our approaches toward education, policy making, staffing, students, and programming in general. When educating children, establishing and following schedules and policies helps them get accustomed to the environment, learn what is expected of them, and feel secure. CPCI has responded to the unique demands of educating children by maintaining highly structured daily schedules and making changes only after careful consideration and planning. Public schools, in a similar form, establish and enforce policies in areas such as dress code, attendance, and performance standards. Adult education programs, on the other hand, often respond to the particularities of individual adults, many of whom have dropped out of highly structured systems that have failed to meet their needs. For them, curriculum, policies, and determiners of success need to be more flexibly determined.

PCAE's adult education model is based on a participatory approach in which adults set their own goals, choose their own classes, dictate much of the curriculum and class rules (if any), and participate in assessing their own progress. In many ways, teachers and students are peers. Students are encouraged to provide direction for their classes and the program. Whereas all three agencies share the goal of helping students take responsibility for themselves and their decisions at appropriate levels of sophistication, the environments that provide for this process are very different and often in opposition.

CPCI structures mealtimes so there are opportunities for children to develop social and communication skills. During August planning, when the full Sunnyside UP staff were refining the schedule for the first week of school, the early childhood staff decided that no meals could be served until parents first learned Head Start rules and the standards for mealtime. Adult educators were uncomfortable with telling parents the right way to eat with their children. The adult educators felt that parents had been eating with their children for years and shouldn't have to be taught how. We felt that it would be appropriate to let parents experience mealtime in the new setting, observe what happened, and then discuss and decide whether or not to develop some rules. This approach was not acceptable to the early childhood educators, who used a more structured approach. Since our colleagues at CPCI had more experience with coordinating meal times in an educational setting, we ended up following their more structured plan. It surprised the early childhood staff that they could not direct the behavior of the parents as easily as the children, and that the parents at Sunnyside UP seemed more resistant than those in other Head Start sites. I suspect that the difference in compliance may be linked to the intensity of parent participation in the program. In most Head Start sites parents visit the class and serve as occasional volunteers but are not a part of the daily program. Parents are asked to model positive attitudes toward food, sample the food themselves even when they do not like it, and encourage their children to do likewise.

Parents in our program who ate the food on a daily basis in the family literacy sites were not able to mask their attitudes about eating cafeteria food, precluding the early childhood staff from meeting their goal of helping children develop positive attitudes around food. At the beginning of the second year, some parents ate with the children on a rotating basis and followed Head Start food policies, but most parents used their lunch time to socialize with other parents or to take time for themselves.

Although parents' complaints about food made the early childhood educators' jobs more difficult because of their desire to encourage positive eating attitudes in the children, the adult educators saw the complaints as an opportunity to incorporate relevant issues into the curriculum. One adult educator used the complaints about cafeteria food as material for lessons in nutrition, math, and writing. The students talked about what they did not like about the food, then analyzed the lunch menu for nutritional content, and found what percentage of the food belonged to each food group. Next, parents did group writing about their impressions of school lunches and put their work on the chalkboard in the form of a letter to the food services department in the public school.

A problem arose when the adult educator did not erase the letter at the end of the day and an early childhood educator came into the class and read it. The early childhood educator got nervous about what would happen if the letter were sent and called the CPCI director. The director in turn became alarmed and felt the adult educator's lesson could jeopardize the program's relationship with the public school. After discussion, the early childhood staff learned that the writing was an example of a participatory approach to curriculum where parents explore their options. The parents had not yet decided whether this letter would be sent; rather, they were using the letter format to clarify their own thoughts. The adult education staff learned that food was a sensitive issue that needed to be handled more delicately in the public school setting. Everyone in the program learned a lesson about the differences in working with children and adults as well as the importance of regular and direct communication.

Conclusion

The field of education is changing as educational providers are being asked to develop partnerships with businesses, social service providers, and community groups to offer a more comprehensive model of education not just for individuals but also for families. Although collaboration is not easy, the rewards are many. Our ability as agencies and individuals to remain flexible will serve us well as we employ the strategies described here, as well as others. In the first year of our partnership, we were able to stretch ourselves as educators and develop a more sophisticated view of the potential of family literacy programs.

Family literacy is not merely encouraging parental involvement in early childhood or public school programs, nor is it simply offering child care for children of parents in adult education classes. It is something different from what any of the collaborators alone could offer. For Sunnyside UP, family literacy came to mean the provision of literacy education in a nurturing atmosphere sensitive to all participants: the learners, their children, and the staff. For us, collaboration meant more than combining efforts; it meant opening ourselves and our vision to new approaches.

CHAPTER 3
Connecting Through Culture Brokers: Promise and Pitfalls

Nora Lewis and Cecelia Varbero

Project LEIF, Learning English through Intergenerational Friendship, is a model program sponsored by the Center for Intergenerational Learning at Temple University's Institute on Aging in Philadelphia, Pennsylvania. LEIF pairs college-age volunteers with non-English-speaking refugee and immigrant elders. Volunteers are trained to go into elders' homes and communities to tutor them in English language and literacy, as well as to help them learn about American society and culture. In return, elders provide tutors with access to a culture and community that is unfamiliar to them, yet exists in their own backyard. The idea for Project LEIF came from a gerontologist who was concerned with age segregation in American society. LEIF was one of many model programs designed to bring young and old together in mutually beneficial ways. Although the organizational base for LEIF was the Institute on Aging, the program began in partnership with the refugee and immigrant communities it serves, and its links to these communities remain vital to the success of the program.

The following discussion focuses on decisions made in program design regarding representation from the participating refugee communities and the unforeseen and far-reaching consequences of those decisions for program operation. We discuss the ramifications of decisions regarding which community organizations and representatives to collaborate with in targeted ethnic communities and the choice of personnel for the bilingual staff assistant position.

Collaboration with Community Leaders

From the very beginning, LEIF program designers established a cooperative relationship with selected, officially recognized leaders of the targeted refugee and immigrant communities. All of these leaders, who held elected or appointed positions in community self-help organizations or senior centers, were asked to sit on an advisory board for LEIF to assist in the initial development of the pilot project. Without exception, all leaders approached were initially very supportive of LEIF and its objectives and offered valuable assistance in establishing LEIF in their communities. However, over time, program staff came to realize that leaders often had behind-the-scenes agendas that, although not directly involving LEIF, could pose a potential risk for conflict with LEIF's need to stay impartial and nonpolitical vis-à-vis community politics. In a few cases, program coordinators had to negotiate novel solutions when community leaders tried to use LEIF in ways that we felt jeopardized our operation.

In the Cambodian community, for example, reliance on a highly placed community leader paradoxically hampered LEIF's efforts to gain access to the community, thereby forcing program staff to develop more grassroots contacts in that community. Yar Sang was the director of a citywide coalition of refugee organizations. (The names of all community leaders and bilingual assistants have been changed.) An articulate man with a Western education and a sophisticated understanding of how American bureaucracy and business work, he was well known in the Southeast Asian communities in general, not just among his own countrymen. LEIF staff assumed that association with a man of Yar Sang's visibility and stature would help draw many elders from the community into the program. In reality, we encountered tremendous difficulty identifying elders who wanted tutors and convincing elders to enroll in the program. Yar Sang was not effective in helping the Cambodian bilingual assistant identify and recruit elders in his own community, especially in the part of the city where his office and our learning center were located. He did, however, help the program gain entry to a newly established Cambodian Buddhist temple as a learning center site in another part of the community.

Puzzled by our difficulty in reaching the community despite Yar Sang's help, program staff began to spend time in the temple, meeting and talking to people from the community who came to visit the Buddhist monks. Out of these conversations, we discovered that many members of the community did not trust Yar Sang, partly due to the fact that he belonged to a different social class with a different educational background and partly due to suspicions about his political beliefs and affiliations. One man went so far as to suggest to one of the authors that Yar Sang was a supporter of the hated Khmer Rouge and reported that others had seen Sang wearing a Khmer Rouge scarf at a public meeting. Although this accusation was patently untrue, it underscored the degree of suspicion about this leader that existed in the minds of many of the community members from a rural background.

This episode had a fortunate resolution because, due to Yar Sang's help in getting LEIF into the Buddhist temple, program staff were able to meet both the monks and an unofficial community leader, all of whom proved invaluable in helping us reach elders in the Cambodian community. However, it revealed to program designers that community leaders who are most visible to Americans because of their English language skills are sometimes removed from the grassroots people they supposedly represent.

In two other very different communities, miscommunication or misunderstanding between the ethnic leaders and program staff over the role that LEIF was expected to play at a learning center led to situations that required the immediate intervention of the program coordinator to ensure continued operation of the program.

For learning centers, Project LEIF uses existing ethnic, religious, or community centers located in neighborhoods where many elders of the target immigrant group live. Thus, LEIF becomes one of many social and human services offered through a given center. At a senior center in the heart of one of Philadelphia's Latino neighborhoods, the director of the center, Mrs. Perez, threatened to end LEIF's access to the center and its elders out of fear that LEIF was jeopardizing funding for other programs by taking elders away from the center. Prior to LEIF's entry into the Latino community, all tutors who met students during normal weekday business hours had been instructed to meet only at the center, and not in the homes. This arrangement appeared to be working satisfactorily from the tutors' perspective, and no problems were apparent to program staff. On several occasions, however, Mrs. Perez called the LEIF learning center staff person or the program coordinator into her office to complain that tutors were keeping elders away from the center by tutoring at home. On each occasion the coordinator investigated but found that only tutors who met their students on weekends or at night, times when the center was closed, were tutoring in the home. These results were reported to Mrs. Perez in person and in writing, but the concern continued to surface with each new batch of tutors assigned to the Latino center. Finally, the LEIF coordinator decided to issue a regular letter to Mrs. Perez at the beginning of each academic semester when new tutors would be coming to her community, assuring her that all tutor-student pairs who met during regular center hours would be required to meet at the center. This letter, plus occasional verbal reassurances, seemed to alleviate fears that LEIF was handicapping rather than helping Mrs. Perez's center.

A second situation at an organization for ethnic Chinese refugees from Southeast Asia revealed similar potential for miscommunication to strain program-community relations. LEIF's goal was to place tutors at the Chinese association to work with individual students. The association, however, saw these tutors as an opportunity to get free teachers for large classes of students (25+ students), thereby saving their limited financial resources for other purposes. As a result, some of the tutors were intimidated into taking on more responsibility than LEIF asked of them. At this point, it became necessary for the LEIF coordinator to step in, not only to protect the goals of the program, but also to guard the rights of the tutors. Fortunately, a direct meeting between the head of LEIF and the head of the Chinese association was sufficient to correct the problem and forestall any future misunderstandings on this issue. Both this experience and the previously mentioned Latino case underscored the crucial point that the relationship between program directors and the community and its leaders could not be taken for granted, but rather needed to be constantly reaffirmed and renegotiated.

Two salient lessons have guided our own thinking from these experiences. First, it is crucial for the director of a community-based program such as Project LEIF to get out into the community personally and regularly, to observe, to meet people, to learn to identify the unofficial leaders of the possible subgroups within the community, and to closely monitor the evolution of program operations from the perspective of those served. Although it is necessary to maintain good relations with official community leaders, those leaders are not always the most effective resources available to support program operation in a community. Second, it is helpful to be clear about what both parties, program and community leaders, are getting from a relationship. This may seem clear at the beginning of a relationship, as it did in the cases of the Latino and ethnic Chinese associations; however, it may be necessary to reaffirm this agreement with each new round of tutor and student recruitment, so that neither party harbors misconceptions about who is to do (or is doing) what.

Selection of Bilingual Assistants

A unique and essential aspect of the LEIF program is its reliance on bilingual assistants for each of the communities it serves. The program's success in great part rests on the bilingual assistant's ability to describe and "know" an ethnic community and thus to become a liaison between the community members and the English-speaking volunteers.

The plan for the program was to choose assistants who had a good command of English in addition to skills in their native language, knowledge of their native culture, access to their community in Philadelphia, and good interpersonal skills. Membership in the community was initially seen as essential for success, but it was discovered that this was not always the case. Identifying people who fit LEIF's profile appeared to be straightforward, but was in fact rather problematic.

In retrospect, the bilingual assistants involved in the program fell into three categories. These designations are based on evaluations of performance of various bilingual assistants over the past five years. There are those who are ethnic outsiders in a particular community but who earn acceptance as members; those who are ethnic members of the community but for reasons to be described cannot reach the entire community; and those who are ethnic members of a community and can cross political, geographic, and socioeconomic boundaries and gain acceptance in the community at large.

Those in our program who were ethnically different from those in the community they served were all Anglo-Americans, working in a well established Latino community. The fact that the community was well established probably enabled our nonnative-Spanish-speaking North American bilingual assistants to interact freely in the community, because community leaders were not threatened by their efforts. All these assistants had near-native levels of fluency in Spanish and had a high degree of motivation for connecting with the community. One bilingual assistant had already worked in other Latino organizations and was conducting research in the Latino community where she had thus become familiar and trusted. She spent many hours in the community center, not only as a LEIF representative, but also building friendships with the elders who "adopted" her. Others, college-age students majoring in Spanish or for personal reasons seeking to learn more about the diverse Latino population in Philadelphia, were equally able to engage members of the community and expand LEIF's presence there. The community, for its part, did not seem to resent or mistrust these "interlopers" and, instead, actually welcomed them eagerly. The warmth and delight that welcomed the bilingual assistants in the Latino community in large part resulted both from the unique and enthusiastic social climate of the Latino culture and the bilingual assistants' language skills and active interest in the community. One drawback, however, was the assistants' relative inability to understand the culture and community from an insider's point of view.

Of those bilingual assistants who were ethnic members of the communities they worked in, not all were uniformly successful in gaining access to the community. The problem was baffling at first, especially since the bilingual assistants appeared to have all the necessary requirements. In one instance, a personable young Cambodian man, a pre-med student, was chosen as a bilingual assistant. He was bright and seemed knowledgeable about Cambodian customs and traditions. Unfortunately, his age was apparently a limiting factor since he was not always regarded as a serious source of needed assistance and had difficulty entering elders' homes as a LEIF representative. Perhaps he was constrained by cultural role expectations in ways that outsiders would not have been. In addition, because of his young age and his limited experience in taking another perspective and comparing himself with Americans and American culture, he was unable to relate culture-bound facts to the mostly American-born tutors. Finally, having left Cambodia as a child, he had never really experienced a traditional celebration and was unable to provide authentic descriptions of typical holiday customs.

Although they were enthusiastic and obviously fluent speakers of the native language of the community, some bilingual assistants encountered barriers based on their socioeconomic group. They were not considered to be at the same economic level as most members of the community and, therefore, were not perceived as able to understand the particular problems of the community. One bilingual assistant came from a middle class family that was able to afford his tuition in an expensive Ivy League university. His family's lifestyle was distinctly beyond the means of most people in his community, who came from rural or peasant backgrounds. This difference seemed sufficient to exclude him from entry into elders' homes.

For others, their residence in a particular geographic area in the community was problematic. In the Cambodian community in Philadelphia, political affiliations and geography go hand-in-hand, and boundaries are clearly delineated. Living in one particular part of the city represents support of a particular political party or belief. The result was that some bilingual assistants were only able to recruit students in one part of the city, while others could only successfully recruit students from among close relatives and friends. One Cambodian bilingual assistant was not able to recruit students outside of her own (South Philadelphia) neighborhood or to gain entry to homes of elders who were unknown to her but who had been recommended to the program through other sources. Only after a well known community spokesperson revealed these geographic boundaries and their significance did the project coordinator understand these limitations.

As part of Project LEIF's search for potential bilingual assistants, the project coordinator sought assistance from leaders in the community suggested by Mutual Assistance Associations (MAAs). [*Editor's note:* See also p. 116 in this volume for more information about MAAs.] These leaders were immensely helpful in explaining the history of the community's presence in the United States and how best to approach people to participate in the program. Through inquiries, Project LEIF was able to find truly successful bilingual assistants.

Our definition of a successful bilingual assistant is a person who may or may not be an ethnic member in the target community but who can cross the invisible (but very real) geopolitical boundaries of the community and interact easily with people in all sectors of the community. Ideal candidates have the unique ability to participate fully in the community and its activities and also look at the community from the vantage point of an outsider, articulating what the community is experiencing and how the community members feel, think, and act. They are uniquely capable not only of gaining access to different families, but also of looking at the community as a whole, as a complete entity with social, cultural, and political needs.

Project LEIF's first bilingual assistant, Yia Lo, epitomized these qualities. Gail Weinstein-Shr, LEIF's founding director, met Yia Lo as a recommended Hmong language teacher for her own ethnographic research in the Hmong community. Weinstein-Shr found this young man from the mountains of Laos to be articulate in explaining Hmong customs, fascinated with cross-cultural comparisons, proud of where he had come from, and anxious to learn more about America and Americans. At the time, Weinstein-Shr was setting up Project LEIF and wasted no time in enlisting Yia's help as a "culture broker"— that is to say, Yia helped Project LEIF get its start by explaining the program to Hmong community elders in ways that convinced them to participate, as well as by teaching new volunteers about his native country and compatriots with humor and insight.

Another outstanding and successful bilingual assistant was a college-age student who was recommended by the head of the MAA coalition. She eventually proved to be an excellent choice because her father was well known and respected in the entire community, enabling her to use his name and contacts to reach families in different parts of the city. This ability to cross borders geographically and politically was enormously helpful. In addition, she was personable, had good interaction skills with both community elders and Americans, had a good understanding of her culture, and was able to explain it to others. While ostensibly her age and her home location would appear to have limited her, her relationship with her father strengthened LEIF's ability to reach the community effectively.

We met another successful bilingual assistant purely by coincidence. At the suggestion of the MAA head, we had begun visiting the Cambodian Buddhist Temple to attempt to set up a learning center. We had been going there regularly to become familiar with the neighborhood and the students when we were approached by Ohm Kor. Ohm Kor turned out to be a reliable and insightful spokesperson for the community, who provided great assistance in identifying students and their needs and in helping Project LEIF to attend effectively to those needs. He was well known and well respected at all levels of the community due to his association with the Buddhist monks and, as an older man himself, was especially trusted by the older generation of Cambodians.

It is only in retrospect that we are able to understand the intricacies of the success of the bilingual assistant selection process. There is no easy way to predict or guarantee that one person will be more suitable than others, and, as so often is the case, pragmatics ultimately govern the decision—the limited pool of potential people, limits enforced by the funding source, and time constraints. The lesson we can derive from these experiences is that asking very pointed and specific questions of potential bilingual assistants can help the director determine who is best qualified for the position. It is important to ask candidates where they live, how many people they know in the ethnic community, how many elders they know, and how they feel about going to new neighborhoods to talk to elders. It is also important to ascertain their degree of participation in traditional cultural events and how well they can describe these traditions to Americans. Isolating these key characteristics can be vital to the success of the program. Sometimes decisions entail a sacrifice of some qualities in favor of others, but knowing which qualities are priorities can make the decision-making process easier and ultimately more effective.

Conclusion

Despite their cross-cultural sensitivity training and experiences working with ethnic communities, the LEIF program designers and administrators tended to view ethnic communities as monolithic; that is, one bilingual assistant and one learning center could effectively represent all the members of one ethnic group, like the Cambodians. In reality, political, religious, socioeconomic, and even geographic divisions within ethnic groups often made it impossible for one bilingual assistant, or one learning center, or one community leader to fulfill the goal of providing ideal service to everyone in a community.

Although it would be ideal to hire bilingual assistants and establish a learning center for each subcommunity, it is not realistic or possible given real-world constraints on funding, time, and staffing. A more realistic alternative is to do two things. First, it is wise initially to limit expectations about reaching a whole community, while striving at the same time to understand the dynamics and boundaries of the target group and subgroups to be served. Second, we found it crucial to develop a network of contacts, including unofficial community leaders, by spending time getting to know people and observing relations and interactions among community members. This makes it possible to learn more about subdivisions within an ethnic community and the best ways to reach their members, and helps generate candidates for bilingual assistants. The more information projects coordinators have, the better they will be equipped to do successful work in a new setting. But the task is never finished. As neighborhoods change, and as key players change, there is always more to learn about those we serve and how to adjust program design for success in a complex setting.

CHAPTER 4
Family Collaboration in Children's Literacy: When Journals Travel Home

Daniel J. Doorn

In a small, rural school along the Rio Grande River in southern New Mexico, the 23 young learners in Charlotte Sánchez's third-grade classroom, the majority of whom were bilingual in Spanish and English, represented a familiar range of literacy interests and experiences. Some loved writing and chose to work on stories during free time; others had to be coaxed and encouraged to write at all. Some welcomed peers to read and write with them; others wanted privacy and warned neighbors of a personal no-peeking policy as they hunched over their products. Some asked for work to take home; others rushed out each day empty-handed, avoiding reminders about an important home assignment.

I observed Charlotte Sanchez's classroom for a good part of a school year, coming first to confer with her on a reading-writing project that she was doing in my graduate practicum course. When she invited me to return in the spring to work in collaboration as a fellow teacher-researcher, apart from any course study, I continued supporting her efforts to enrich the classroom conditions for literacy development within an overall supportive environment of second language growth. I gathered observational records as she tried to expand the use of good literature with the children and structure more conference time with them as they wrote. Over time, the signs of growth among individuals were clear and encouraging, but many still showed caution and uncertainty about being readers and writers.

Of special concern was the evidence that, for many students, the need to write and read did not extend very far. The borders of literacy uses seemed drawn around a limited field. We noticed, for example, that many students drew upon the same imaginary-world topics week after week when planning new stories. Unless directed in an assignment, few showed interest in writing to inform class-mates about their wider world of experiences. We also noticed that in their off-task discussions, the students shared a rich variety of out-of-school exploits and family concerns at home, but they did not go on to explore them further in writing.

We wondered about the need for change, adjustments, on new initiatives. Although I encouraged Mrs. Sánchez to be patient in her ongoing attempts to enhance writers' workshop activities and add more opportunities for writing across the curriculum, we both sensed a need to explore new ways of expanding the children's writing experiences. How could we help the children see new options in finding topics, setting purposes, and collaborating in their writing? In particular, we wondered about ways they could explore those options at home.

Our response was to begin a new venture of shared learning experiences. We invited students to use a take-home journal during the remaining 12 weeks of the school year. Up to that point, they had not used any type of personal journals, other than folders of collected in-class writing. The initiative began with a desire to pursue a literacy agenda with three subgoals and related questions.

1. Increase social interaction.
Can the children do more sharing with others at home?

2. Expand student responsibility in contributing to literacy activities.
Can they bring in topics of interest from home for reading and writing?

3. Promote greater uses of written language in all learning events.
Can they write with and for the family?

We knew it would be a challenge for us and for the children to explore the possibilities by use of a journal that traveled back and forth between home and the classroom. Grappling with the practical aspects of structuring a new journal component into the daily curriculum was the first challenge. The most important challenge, however, was to see how the journals could prompt new opportunities for family collaboration, and how the sharing of those home experiences in the classroom could enhance literacy growth for the whole community of young writers.

In a search for answers to our project questions, I frequently came to write, watch, and learn along with the students. Mrs. Bowers, the student teacher assigned to the class that spring, was especially committed to nurturing the project on days I could not come. She joined me in reflecting on the language stories and literacy insights that emerged each week. Together we gathered anecdotal records, guided peer conferences, and celebrated the discoveries that the children were making. In the following stories, I describe our sense of distinct appreciation for the lessons we learned, and celebrate the way in which the students explored and found value in sharing their traveling journals. The stories are not intended to describe all of the procedures for implementing journals, and readers interested in knowing more about the practical aspects may want to explore the list of resources given at the end of this chapter.

This chapter begins with some stories about the early steps of prompting collaboration and supporting the use of journals taken out of the classroom. The early lessons taught us patience, reminding us that student ownership takes time to develop. The students also showed us process insights. Their journal entries were sparked, at first, by questions raised among peers at school, but later were increasingly enriched through talks with families at home. Next, the chapter highlights a milestone occurring midway through the project, with an account of one child's distinctive breakthrough with his journal. It was a compelling reference point for understanding how the project was attracting interest and encouraging participation among all the children, especially the more hesitant writers. Finally, I describe the lessons we learned in sustaining the value of a take-home journal over time. Many of the students sensed that they had just begun to tap into community life situations that deserved reflections in their journals. As listeners to their stories, we ourselves increased our desire to find out more about the collaborative roles of the children's family and friends at home.

Getting Started: "We're Learners at Home, Too"

I started the home-school journal project by bringing my own journal to the third-grade classroom. A picture of an unhealthy tree with a question about how to rid it of damaging insects was my first entry. My next entry was a draft of a thank-you note to a friend who had recently shown me his amazing rock collection. These two entries, displayed in a brightly colored folder, were examples of my using a journal to record observations of concerns at home. After listening to my entries, the students were asked to think about the potential of starting their own journals. They were asked to think about what they could record at home that they could not very well do at school.

Suggestions the first day included writing songs, practicing math, and asking parents questions about specific community problems. Two of the questions that went home in many journals that evening were: Why is there garbage all over our yard? and What are some bad bugs and good bugs?

When the new journals, encased in orange folders, returned the following day, we were eager to see the first entries. Several children returned with their questions unanswered. They were the wait-and-see group; they seemed to need more demonstrations from peers before writing entries on their own. A few of the boys returned with drawings in response to the take-home questions. They were the free-spirited artists; they were not going to quickly forsake pictures for text writing. More than half of the students did bring in answers to the questions, resulting from talks with family, and several even included new questions to further challenge the class. Most of this group responded to the garbage question. One boy reported that he had thought of a new question for the class while he was walking to school that morning and had written it when he arrived at school: "Why are the [irrigation] ditches have dirty water?"

One child who especially helped us learn our first lessons on collaborating was Tomás. He had one single word printed on his first blank page: *bakita*. He was pleased to tell his sharing group that *bakita*, or lady bugs, were really helpful bugs in the fruit trees. His dad had assured him that every garden needed them. In their group discussion, classmates agreed that *bakita* were indeed lady bugs; they did their work by eating other bugs, and they were fun to catch. No one in the group was quite sure about Tomás's spelling of the word. For a moment, when the whole class was asked to help, it seemed that no one knew the answer. Someone then remembered that the newest and quietest member of the class, Angel, who had recently come from Mexico, might know the spelling. She did! When she wrote out *vaquita* and passed it on to Tomás, the whole class joined him in a smile of appreciation.

In time, we all came to realize that others in the class had surprising ways of helping. Angel went on to record a favorite Spanish folktale in her journal, told to her one evening by her mother and grandmother. It was a story about valuing frogs' appetite for mosquitoes. The whole class encouraged her to read it in Spanish, after which her friends made a translation copy in English for others to read again.

On the first day of the project, we set up a small journal center (see Figure 1) conveniently placed by the main exit door in the room. Students could drop off and pick up their journals here in a plastic storage crate. On the wall above the table, Mrs. Bowers maintained two types of charts. One chart was for posting new questions that students felt were worth asking family or friends at home. She changed it about every two weeks to keep up with all the questions. In many cases, however, students stated their questions orally during the afternoon journal conferences and wrote them in their journals.

Figure 1. Small journal center in classroom

The other chart was an open-ended list of ways to use the journals. During most sessions, someone pointed out some new way we could record in our journals. One day, for example, Mrs. Bowers honored Vanessa's latest idea, "Interview a neighbor," by adding it to the reminder list of journal options posted by the door. By the end of the year, we had recorded 15 different ways, certainly fewer than we had actually tried out.

Ways We Can Use Our Home-School Journal

1. Making poems: Writing our own; copying ones we like.

2. Writing stories: True ones; imaginary ones.

3. Making a list of our interests.

4. Writing questions to ask our families.

5. Drawing pictures: Things we see at home; things we do at home.

6. Collecting pictures from magazines and newspapers and writing about them.

7. Writing reports about some new information we found out at home.

8. Writing about talking to a neighbor—An interview.

9. Writing about a talk to an imaginary neighbor.

10. Listening to someone tell a story and then write about it.

11. Copying something interesting we find at home.

12. Inventing your own math problems at home.

13. Writing notes to remember things to do at home.

14. Making up jokes.

15. Telling about miracles and amazing stories we hear.

Maintanence of the list stopped at number 15. The teacher admitted that she forgot about recording new suggestions, but the students continued to report other good ideas. One was the use of the journal on trips, recording experiences shared with the family while traveling.

During the first few weeks of the program, we realized that this center played an important visual role. The students could see the freedom they had to make choices about writing topics and could keep track of each other's ideas for new uses for the journals.

We certainly had hopes about how the children might come to value the journals, and we learned early on that they uncovered distinctively playful ways of writing in them. One week, thanks to Ramón and his list of wrestlers seen on television, a new wave of playful entries began pouring in. Many students made lists of their favorites. Lists of favorite sports figures and teams came first, followed by movies, colors, and animals. A few seemed not to tire of the list making. Three weeks later, they were still uncovering new categories of favorite things.

One valuable lesson I learned early in the process came from observing Mrs. Bowers inviting the students to get out their home-school journals. Hearing the enthusiasm in her voice and seeing the way she clutched her own journal, I realized how important it was to the students that the teacher enjoyed being a learner right along with them. A shared sense of responsibility for learning made the after-lunch journal routine a very welcome time for everyone in the class.

Two events pushed us to encourage the students to contact others about their topics of interest. One came in response to students bringing in their lists of favorite things. We asked them how their parents or grandparents might have composed such lists as children. Within a few days we had our answers. One boy was particularly eager to read aloud his journal notes on his father's youthful interests. Within his sharing group, he treated his peers to a few lines from his father's favorite radio song, "Cha-cha-cha," and other memories his father had told him about—his best-liked picture (himself in a cowboy suit) and his most-watched television show ("Bozo the Clown"). Fascination with the past seemed to touch the whole class that week.

Because so many students brought in intriguing records of interviews with parents, Mrs. Bowers asked students to recopy their lists on strips of paper and post them on a sheet of butcher paper for all to see. It was a time when the journals alone were not sufficient for sharing a sudden rush of family-life discoveries, and new types of writing were generated.

Another opportunity for extending collaboration came in response to Olivia's journal. One day she brought in an entry that read, "I need help nitting." Mrs. Bowers was first to notice Olivia sharing the entry among a group of friends, who were interested in knowing what she wanted to make. At the end of the journal conference time, we agreed that Olivia's call for help should go beyond her small peer group. The following notice went up on the "Attention Poster" before students went home that day.

Class, I need help in knitting (or crocheting).

If you are interested in helping Olivia, write

a note in your journal. Ask if your Mom or

Grandma might like to teach her.

We were really pleased, as was Olivia, when another classmate, Vanessa, brought in her journal entry two days later; it read, "Grandma can. Olivia can come over so you can show us how to croshay." Slowly but surely classmates were letting each other know that journals would be treated with authentic reader responses.

Spreading Involvement

The growing awareness of a supportive writing community began to attract the more reluctant writers in class. We noticed that they were ready to step in and see how peers and the teachers would respond to their efforts. One of those reluctant students was Edgar, a boy who often distanced himself from others and their ideas for the journals, preferring to sketch monsters and machines in his journal. One day after Edgar listened to his journal group talk about things they could make, he noted that he could use a piece of cloth to make a rabbit. A few were curious about how it was done; a couple expressed doubts that he could do it. I had been listening in on their conversation, and I encouraged Edgar to write himself a note in his journal, reminding him to show the class how to create a cloth rabbit. Admittedly, I was doubtful that he would accept our invitation, and I did not stay to watch his response.

What a surprise it was to read Edgar's journal at the end of the week when Mrs. Bowers and I reviewed everyone's entries. He had recorded his very first written entry, beyond the naming of his monster drawings. It was simple, but it marked a new willingness to join the group. It read:

not.
1. toul
2. breng to shool   [Translation: note. 1. towel 2. bring
3. sho the class ho   to school 3. show the class how]

As we reviewed the early journal collaborations, arising both at home and at school, we were most struck by the need to give students a structured, predictable time to talk about their entries in groups, allowing others to respond to the ideas they were most interested in. Many new inquiries arose from these after-lunch conferences, but none was more touching than the question posed one day by Melissa.

After listening to her group discuss a range of topics, including illnesses, grandparents, and life in the past, Melissa wrote a question in her journal that she had never thought to ask before. She told her group that she had never seen her grandfather because he had died before she was born. Her written question was, "Why did my grandpa die?" That night she asked her question at home and learned the answer. Her journal entry, read to her group the next day, described the accident that had taken her grandfather's life.

Milestones Along the Way: "I Want to Join You Guys, Too"

On one particular Monday, as the students eagerly pulled out their folders stored in the crate by the main door, I wondered who might be bringing in a new type of home experience that could expand our ideas for writing. As I had come to expect surprises, I tended to show a good deal of eagerness in starting the routine conferences. I quickly accepted an invitation to join one of the small working groups at a table designated for the sharing of new stories from home.

For a few minutes I listened to Tomás, who was ignoring a story he had written at home in preference to reading his list of favorite animals again. As I glanced up, I suddenly noticed another boy, Daniel, subtly trying to get my attention from across the room. Something was very different about this usually shy, often withdrawn, hesitant-to-share young boy. His eyes were dancing today; his whole way of moving was noticeably animated. The surprise for me, and probably for him, too, was that he was actually taking the lead to let me and our group know about his story—not loudly, as the others were doing, but certainly with a similar sense of urgency. He was beaming his request, using his eyes to say, "I can hardly wait to show you what I did at home this weekend."

For the next 30 minutes, our group gave its full attention to Daniel and his story, "My Family's Trip to Mexico." Because he struggled with fluency in reading, his friends decided to join him, taking turns reading and rereading the text. At one point, two class-mates leaned cheek-to-cheek over his shoulders and another hunched on the table in front of him, all voicing a part of the text in unison. The group also took time to question him for more information and to comment on events that surprised us all. I am sure his peers were as amazed as I was by Daniel's writing that day. He had never writ-ten any text of such length and with such fascinating details. But there it was, complete with a drawing of the family car dodging deer on a highway in Mexico.

Figure 2. One student's story

Daniel did not simply recount his family's activities while visiting relatives over the border. Instead, he described and commented on two special memories: seeing so many deer killed along one stretch of the highway and smelling such polluted air, which afflicted the children living in one of the urban areas of Mexico. Unlike the journal entries shared over the preceding weeks by the other children in the class, Daniel had shaped his writing around specific events, describing them clearly and recording the reflections that he and his family shared after returning home. He gave us a very different kind of writing to ponder and linger over. He showed his peers a new and important reason to write: to work out our reflections on things in life that seem so troubling at times.

One more surprise came after the group shifted away to other journal conferences that formed freely during the afternoon time block. Daniel quietly confided to me that it was his cousin who had actually put the story down on paper. Daniel had called him over to the house that weekend and had asked him to transcribe as he dictated the words. Daniel knew he could not write his story the way he wanted to tell it, but after four weeks of observing others share their journal entries, he was determined to find a way to join his classmates as a full-fledged journal writer, even if that meant getting someone else to handle his pencil.

Later that day, when Mrs. Bowers and I reviewed our observations, we realized that the earlier rounds of journal sharing were beginning to make a strong impact on the whole class, attracting even the hesitant writers to bring in stories from home. Daniel's story helped us appreciate another important fact: Any one of the children, even the more reluctant and less confident writers, could come with literacy surprises from home. Daniel had given the class a story with adventure and, at the same time, revealed his willingness to take risks and to use writing to evaluate his own experiences. Daniel had explored literacy to meet his personal needs and had modeled the possibilities of more reflective writing for the whole community of young writers in his class.

Closing Thoughts: "We Can Take Our Journals Anywhere"

Toward the end of the project, I came across a little note, written just for me in Anna's journal. It must have been fun to slip in a secret message, but it was probably hard for her to wait until the end of the week when I would discover it in my review of everyone's journals. Anna's note read, "Dear Dan, My mom said I could take my journal to Albuquerque." She thought that was the greatest of her new ideas, using her journal to record what she saw and did on a family trip to the big city up north. She even thought she might work on a new story if there was time. Anna's interest in taking her journal on the road showed us how students were indeed relating the process of writing to many different events in their lives.

After many weeks of observing the journal writing, we decided to elicit student evaluations. I opened one after-lunch session by noting that students in nearby schools did not have home-school journals but might be curious to know more about them. I then invited the students to write letters to point out the benefits of their journals and encourage others to try journal writing.

As the letters emerged, we were fascinated by the ways students practiced the art of being persuasive with an understanding, inter-personal touch. One example had an amazing claim, "I hope you start a journal. It's funer than play Nintendo." Another showed real consideration, "I will lend you a pencil and a pen." Many shared hopes for finding similar interests, "I hope you are going to writ about animals." Several emphasized appreciation for a freedom of choice and an expectation of class response:

> *You could put all the things you want to. Then when you bring the journal to school you say to the teacher you want to share. Then you go to the front of the class and read. If you write jokes they will laugh.*

In early May, I had to stop attending the class; Mrs. Bowers, the student teacher, had to leave for other university demands; and Mrs. Sánchez had to reschedule the days' events for the closing of the school year. Decisions about further use of the journals that spring were placed in the hands of the students. It was hard to let go of our support role, yet we appreciated learning so much that would help us continue the project in the fall. We also knew we would greatly miss the sharing times with students because, above all else, we had come to view the project as one of joining others in making new discoveries—about themselves, about their peers, and about their families.

In my last week with the class, I reflected on the children's literacy growth, hoping to see more than increased fluency, quantity of writing, and accuracy. I wondered if there were signs that the students were proceeding on a path toward using journals for more reflective and creative responses to all their learning experiences. Indeed, there were such signs, and one example was most endearing. Tommy, the resident champ of list making, made a very different type of entry in the last week. His entry from home was a poem, drawn from all the animal names he had been listing in his journal. He read it for his classmates as a poetic talk he had with himself.

Animals,

Animals.

Animals are the best.

So why don't you be

a scientist of animals.

It is so fun.

Animals,

Animals.

The poem was a small but exciting step forward: finding in writing new steps of action for the future. With the poem, Tommy had extended the meaning of his list-writing experiences. He realized he did not have to end his personal interest in animals; he could sustain it. In being a reflective writer, he was learning to look ahead, beyond present experiences, and see new possibilities for growth steps in his life.

Of all the accounts shared in the classroom that spring, I realized that we were just beginning to hear a much larger story, a richly textured narrative created by other co-authors, co-readers, and co-illustrators, who were sharing the children's adventures of literacy growth outside school. As the children energized our classroom with the stories they brought from home, they gave us hints about the times, places, and ways in which they interacted with family and community members. The clues of collaboration were clear enough to give us a sense of the roles these participants played beyond the classroom during the past three months. They worked with the children as interviewees, informants, encouragers, storytellers, and storyreaders. Much of the details of their roles, however, remained untold, and I left the class with a strong desire to learn more about the home interactions that had helped shape the stories brought to the classroom. One of our plans for uncovering more of the whole story of home collaboration next year is to do home visits to interview parents and ask them to keep records of their interactions with the children.

Our exploratory project with home-school journals confirmed that growth in writing comes with extensive amounts of caring social interaction with others. From the bilingual group of children in Mrs. Sánchez's class, we learned the value of widening the circle of participants who can collaborate with young writers in multicultural communities. The added family voices at home supported the children in expanding the content of their writing and valuing a greater variety of purposes for writing about their lives. Hearing the encouragement of those voices at home being passed on among peers at school, how could we not continue exploring opportunities for home collaboration for these young children?

Resources

The following resources may be of interest to readers who want to know more about the development of literacy among young writers. These resources provide stories of students using different types of journals, collaborating with peers in writing conferences, developing their storytelling voices, sharing reading at home, or, more generally, taking new reflective steps into the world of literacy.

Fulwiler, T. (Ed.). (1987). *The journal book*. Portsmouth, NH: Heinemann.

Goodman, K., Bridges, L., & Goodman, Y. (Eds.). (1991). Collected articles from *The Whole Language Catalog*. Santa Rosa, CA: American School.

Hudelson, S. (1989). *Write on: Children writing in ESL*. Englewood Cliffs, NJ: Prentice Hall Regents and Center for Applied Linguistics.

Mikkelson, N. (1990). Toward greater equity in literacy education: Storymaking and non-mainstream students. *Language Arts, 67,* 556-566.

Parsons, L. (1989). *Response journals*. Portsmouth, NH: Heinemann.

Peyton, J.K. (1990). Beginning at the beginning: First grade ESL students learn to write. In A.M. Padilla, H.H. Fairchild, & L.M. Valdez (Eds.), *Bilingual education: Issues and strategies* (pp. 195-218). Newbury Park, CA: Sage.

Peyton, J.K., & Reed, L. (1991). *Dialogue journal writing with nonnative English speakers: A handbook for teachers*. Alexandria, VA: Teachers of English to Speakers of Other Languages.

Strickland, D. (1991). Making connections: Home and school. *Teachers Networking: The Whole Language Newsletter, 10*(1), 8-11.

Urzúa, C. (1986). A children's story. In P. Rigg & D.S. Enright (Eds.), *Children and ESL: Integrating perspectives* (pp. 93-112). Washington, DC: Teachers of English to Speakers of Other Languages.

Wollman-Bonilla, J. (1991). *Response journals*. New York: Scholastic.

Curriculum: Drawing on Learner Strengths

All learners, regardless of the amount and type of formal education they have had, have rich stories to tell and gifts of strength to pass on to others. To many educators who have worked with immigrant and culturally diverse learners, this has been proven over and over again. To educators and noneducators who have a pluralistic view of people in general, this statement corresponds with a vague feeling about the strengths of the human spirit. The time has come to further disseminate information that both celebrates and illustrates learner strengths and shows the rich potential of learners' knowledge and experience as a point of departure for curriculum, lesson, and activity development.

Family and intergenerational literacy programs see the need to create their own curricula and materials in part because of a lack of appropriate materials on the market, in part because of the uniqueness of their programs and participants, and in part because of respect for the knowledge that learners bring to the programs. Educators in family literacy programs have found that while it is helpful to look at the work of other projects as a guide, the curriculum that is most useful and relevant to each project must be developed with participation by learners, specifically for the learners in that project (Weinstein-Shr, 1992). There are no recipes for quick and easy lesson development. Yet, individually and collectively, the learners themselves provide the substance of the curriculum.

The Refugee Women's Alliance, a nonprofit organization in Seattle, Washington, with the mission of helping refugee women achieve self-sufficiency, developed a Family Story Curriculum Project. The project was built on storytelling activities in which participants remembered and told folktales from their native countries. Judy de Barros (1991) writes, "Everyone has stories. Everyone has a past. Sharing our past is a way to communicate in the present."

At Streamwood Elementary School in Elgin, Illinois, a family literacy program has been developed as part of an extensive parent involvement program. Curricula are designed by the parents for their children. The parents and children tell stories and make and publish books of their stories for their families and the school library. Lois Sands, the school principal, advocates and supports literacy-rich home environments through many activities such as sending children home with books for parents to read to them, book sales where parents are able to find storybooks in their native language, and journal writing in which the children write journals at school and take them home periodically to share with their parents (Sands, 1991).

The chapters that follow contain detailed examples of how specific programs have constructed curricula based on learner strengths. In "From Deficit to Strength: Changing Perspectives on Family Literacy," Elsa Auerbach raises the issues involved in drawing on learner strengths and articulates the fallacies of the school transmission models so often used in literacy curricula. She discusses theoretical perspectives and gives practical examples to make her statement that advocates problem posing and participatory curriculum development. The article documents a family literacy project based on a model that is both informed by research and attentive to participants' strengths and voices.

In "Memories of Mami in the Family Literary Class," Loren McGrail describes how a writing process approach can give birth to an active and thriving participatory curriculum for literacy. A detailed discussion of a publishing project by the "Mamis" (mommies) exemplifies four steps of participatory writing, which she describes as 1) listening to and finding themes, 2) exploring themes or topics, 3) extending literacy to action inside and outside the classroom, and 4) evaluating learning and actions. McGrail shows how these steps coincide with the different aspects of the writing process.

In "Literacy from Within: The Project FIEL Curriculum," Ana Huerta-Macías describes a curriculum developed for parents and children who participate together in family literacy classes. The curriculum uses a participatory, whole languages (Spanish and English) framework and evolves continually with input from and interaction with the adults and children involved. Macías gives examples of how the parents' and children's knowledge become integral parts of lessons, and she addresses the social-contextual effects of building on this knowledge.

In "Our Stories to Transform Them: A Source of Authentic Literacy," Maritza Arrastía demonstrates how "our predominantly oral community attains literacy in a way that affirms and transforms our existing culture." Through the stories the participants tell, they have an inexhaustible source of learning material and an invaluable tool for transforming their stories to "become makers, shapers, and protagonists of our own life tales." Arrastía not only describes the process used for storytelling in a literacy group, but also addresses from a personal perspective many of the issues involved in multicultural education.

References

de Barros, J. (1991). Storytelling project: Unpublished manuscript. (ERIC Document Reproduction Service No. ED 359 838)

Sands, L. (1991). *Streamwood Elementary parent involvement project.* Unpublished manuscript.

Weinstein-Shr, G. (1992). *Family and intergenerational literacy in multilingual families. ERIC Q&A.* Washington, DC: Center for Applied Linguistics, National Clearinghouse on Literacy Education. (ERIC Document Reproduction Service No. ED 321 624)

CHAPTER 5

From Deficit to Strength: Changing Perspectives on Family Literacy

Elsa Roberts Auerbach

Ten years ago, the term family literacy was virtually unknown. Today it has become a buzzword in educational policy and planning circles. Initiatives such as the Barbara Bush Family Literacy Foundation, Even Start legislation, and Title VII Family Literacy projects have put the concept on the front burner. Yet, despite the intensity of public attention focused on family contributions to children's literacy development, there is a pervasive gap between research and practice, there are widely diverging perspectives on parental roles and program models, and, most importantly, the voices of language minority parents are largely absent from the debate. This article recounts the experience of one family literacy project that attempted to make sense of these conflicting perspectives and to develop a model both informed by research and responsive to participants' realities and voices.

In 1987, three community-based adult literacy programs in the greater Boston area—the Jackson-Mann Community School, the Community Learning Center, and the Cardinal Cushing Center for the Spanish Speaking—embarked on a collaborative project with the University of Massachusetts-Boston to develop a participatory model of English family literacy. The project, funded by the Office of Bilingual Education and Minority Languages Affairs (OBEMLA), Title VII, was one of many designed to provide English literacy instruction to parents of children in bilingual education programs. Whereas some family literacy projects provide joint parent-child instruction, this model targeted adults and established ESL (and, in one case, Spanish) literacy classes at each of the three sites.

At the beginning of the project, the family literacy field was considerably less developed than it is today. Thus, we were faced with the question, "What is family literacy?" The fact that there were no commonly agreed-upon answers to this question turned out to be an advantage. It forced us to look critically at existing family literacy program models in light of ethnographic research on family contributions to the literacy development of children from different socioeconomic backgrounds and cultures. More importantly, it prompted us to listen carefully to what our students had to say, to learn from them, and to investigate their own family literacy contexts with them.

Current Models

As we looked at existing family literacy programs, we found that the predominant model often seemed to be one in which "schools identify problems, determine goals/program needs, and then ask the home for help, but only on the schools' terms" (Davies, 1980, p.72). Although the form of these programs varied, what unified them was the view that the values and practices of the school should be transmitted to the home via the parents. The goal often seemed to be to transform home contexts into sites for mainstream literacy interactions and to inculcate parents with the skills and behaviors necessary to interact on the school's terms.

The direction of this predominant model, which I call the "transmission of school practices" model (Auerbach, 1989, p. 168), is *from the schools→to the parents→to the children*. In this model, curriculum developers start with needs and practices identified by so-called experts, often school personnel, and design curricula to enable parents to conform to these expectations. Very often, these expectations take the form of teaching parents how to carry out school-like activities in the home, such as reading report cards, and of training parents in "effective parenting" (for example, how to discipline children). The culture of the school and the established ways of schooling remain intact, unchallenged; it is the parents who must adjust to the schools rather than the schools accommodating the cultural diversity of the students.

Questionable Assumptions

As we began to investigate the ethnographic literature about family contributions to literacy development, it became clear to us that the transmission-of-school-practices model rests on a number of questionable assumptions, such as the following, not borne out by research.

1. Language minority children come from literacy-impoverished home environments, where literacy is neither valued nor developed. According to this assumption, parents do not read, write, or provide positive models of literacy use for their children.

2. Family literacy development takes place through a one-way transfer of skills from parents to children. The parents' role is to teach children either directly or indirectly through a trickle-down effect. Conversely, if parents do not do this, illiteracy is passed from parents to child, creating an "intergenerational cycle of illiteracy."

3. What accounts for success in literacy acquisition is families doing school-like literacy tasks together: parents helping with homework, reinforcing skills work with children, and so forth. The model assumes that parents need guidance in setting up regular, structured, and monitored literacy tasks in the home.

4. Language minority children are disadvantaged by their parents' inability to communicate with them in English, and the more English parents are able to use in the home, the more they will be able to support their children's English literacy development.

5. What schools are already doing is fine, and what is needed is more support for school practices at home, because (it is claimed) what happens at home is the primary determinant of literacy acquisition.

6. Finally, this model rests on the assumption that contextual factors, such as socioeconomic conditions, cultural differences, and family structures, are problematic obstacles that stand in the way of literacy development. They must be addressed outside class as a precondition of or supplement to instruction.

Taken together, these assumptions paint a picture of family inadequacy. The dominant image is one of disease: A raging illiteracy epidemic has been uncovered that originates in unhealthy family environments and can only be cured or eradicated by enlightened social intervention. The danger of this picture is that, under the guise of well intentioned altruism, it projects a new version of the deficit hypothesis, once again blaming marginalized people for their own marginalization. As a result, it ultimately may drive away the very people it is designed to help, because it focuses on their inadequacies and prescribes solutions for them.

Counterevidence

As we examined the assumptions of the predominant model in light of ethnographic research and listened to what our students were saying about their own family literacy contexts, a very different picture of how to approach family literacy began to emerge. While our findings are more fully explored elsewhere (Auerbach, 1989), I touch on the main ones here, first providing counterevidence for each of the above assumptions and then suggesting implications for program design and including the voices of family literacy class participants in each case.

First, study after study shows that language minority families often place enormous value on literacy (McKay & Weinstein-Shr, 1993). Even under the most adverse socioeconomic conditions, they use a wide range of literacy materials and practices for a variety of purposes, audiences, and situations in their homes (Delgado-Gaitan, 1987; Díaz, Moll, & Mehan, 1986; Snow, 1987; Taylor & Dorsey-Gaines, 1988). As Snow (1987) says, "It seems then that explanations implicating the absence of literacy in low-income homes as the source of children's reading failure are simply wrong" (p. 127). In fact, parents support their children in a variety of ways. Over and over, our own students provided evidence of this, as the following quote from a parent demonstrates:

> I help my kids by staying together with them, by talking to them. I help them by confronting them and telling them what's wrong or right just as they do me. I help them when they need a favor or money, just as they do me. It's just like you scratch my back, I scratch your back with my family.

Program implication:

Given the range of materials and literacy practices in the homes of minority families, it may be more productive for family literacy programs to investigate actual home and community practices with students in order to build on strengths rather than assume inadequacies and focus on weaknesses.

Second, as the quote from the parent above indicates, a two-way support system characterizes the literacy interactions of many immigrant families rather than a one-way transfer of knowledge and skills. In fact, the above passage was written through a collaborative mother-daughter language experience process with the mother telling the daughter what she wanted to say and the daughter helping the mother write it. In immigrant families, the parents are often dependent on the children rather than vice versa, and the power of working with parents may be that it reduces this dependency, thus freeing the children to attend to their own development. A model predicated on the assumption of unilateral parent-to-child literacy assistance neither corresponds to the reality of many immigrant families nor facilitates literacy development of parent or child. Role reversals between parent and child, as well as strategies for addressing any problems they may generate, can become the content or vehicle for language and literacy work in classes for parents. For example, the following dialogue between a mother (Lucia) and child (María) was developed by a teacher in our project, Andrea Nash, to elicit class discussion and critical analysis of the complex interaction among language, attitudes, and family dynamics:

Lucia: *Vámonos, pues.*

María: I don't want to go with you.

Lucia: *¿Porqúe no?*

María: Because you always talk in Spanish. It sounds stupid. When you speak Spanish, everyone knows we come from Puerto Rico. Why don't you talk to me in English?

Lucia: *Tu familia habla español. Debe sentirse orgullosa de tus raíces.*

María: English is better. All my friends speak English. Anyway, I don't understand Spanish.

The teacher can guide a discussion through which students share experiences, discuss the social and contextual roots of home dynamics, and strategize together about how to deal with them (see Auerbach, 1992).

Program implication:

Rather than assuming a unilateral parent-to-child transfer of skills, it may be more appropriate to investigate actual family support systems and literacy dynamics with parents, focusing on shared literacy and facilitating parents' independent literacy development.

Third, longitudinal studies of the family contexts of successful readers show that it is not separate, add-on school-like activities that account for literacy acquisition, but rather literacy activities that are integrated in socially significant ways into the ongoing daily lives of learners (Heath, 1983; Snow, 1987; Taylor, 1983). What is important is not so much direct literacy instruction by parents, but the diversity of contexts for literacy use and the role of literacy in accomplishing meaningful family transactions. The following excerpt (discussed more fully in Auerbach & McGrail, 1991) shows how one student began to use writing to explore issues of concern to her: in this case, the emotionally loaded issue of language choice in her family.

My husband speaks to me in English. And I understand everything he says to me but I don't speak to him in English because I don't want him to see my mistakes because I am embarrassed in front of him. He speaks to me in English and I speak to him in Spanish. Only I speak in English to my daughter and the people in the street or when I go to the hospital or my daughter's school because her teacher speaks in English. (p. 107)

Program implication:

Rather than emphasizing specific school-like tasks to be done in the home, programs should support the diversification of contexts for and interactions surrounding literacy-related experiences, so that literacy becomes socially significant in addressing participants' day-to-day concerns.

Fourth, as the student suggests in the quote above, the question of language choice in the home is both important and complex. We may be doing our students a profound disservice by equating family literacy with *English* family literacy and simplistically promoting the use of English in the home. Increasingly, research evidence indicates that the quality of linguistic interaction between parents and children is more important in supporting academic development than the language of that interaction (Cummins, 1981; Wells, 1986). Because parents can negotiate meaning best in their first language, they should be supported in doing so. Further, a solid basis of development in the first language is critical for acquisition of the second language (Cummins, 1981). Finally, a positive attitude toward the first language facilitates acquisition of the second language. The following transcription from a conversation in one of our classes indicates the richness of discussion that is possible when students are given the opportunity to explore questions of the role of the first language in family life (rather than having English family literacy prescribed). In her journal, the teacher, Madeline Rhum, subtitled this discussion (which she had taped and transcribed), "Culture, to change or not to change?" It was prompted when she asked students how they felt about the tension between learning the new language and culture versus maintaining the old.

François: You need to change and learn the language.

Vasilios: What happens when you go to church? What language does the priest speak?

François: If my children want to go to American church, that's OK. They can go.

Vasilios: My kids went to American school during the day and to Greek school in the afternoon. They read, speak, and write both languages.

María: My sister's kids only speak English. They don't understand anything in Creole. I used to tell my nephew in Creole, "You're ugly." My nephew didn't understand anything. Everyone laughed except him. He told his mom that he didn't like it when he was at my house. Everyone spoke Creole and laughed at him. He told his mom that he wanted to learn to speak Creole. The next time I saw him, I said the same thing to him and he said, "Don't call me ugly." He had learned to speak Creole; his mother taught him.

Hilda: In my family, all the kids are bilingual. My two daughters work downtown. They get good money because they are bilingual. I have two kids still at home. I read Spanish books to them.

Elsa: To keep the language is important. We have to speak our language at home. Tell our stories. Tell them about the situation in our country. You don't know if you will go back one day.

María: You have to explain everything about the old country to them.

Gebre: To keep the language is very important. Two of our kids were born in Sudan, and their native language is Arabic. I speak Arabic at home with my wife. I'm trying to teach them Oromo too. I buy cassettes and record something (in my language) and play the tape for them.

Vasilios: Use the tapes to tell stories.

Program implication:

All this evidence points to the need to support maintenance and use of the first language in the home, emphasize the quality of interactions, and support first-language literacy development when necessary.

Counterevidence to the fifth assumption, that schools are doing an adequate job and it is home factors that account for illiteracy, comes from a number of sources. In case studies of home and school contexts of refugee children, Urzúa (1986) found that several children with supportive home environments made little progress with reading and writing, whereas others with seemingly less conducive home environments approached literacy with eagerness and made great progress. The former students were in classrooms that emphasized a reductionist subskills (spelling and phonics) approach to literacy, while the latter were in a whole language classroom where children were encouraged to write every day and where subskills were subordinated to making meaning.

On a grander scale, the Harvard Families and Literacy Study found that in the early grades "either literate, stimulating homes or demanding, enriching classrooms can make good readers" (Snow, 1987, p. 128), but after Grade 3, even children with strong home literacy environments fall back if school factors are weak. Further, this study found that the extent to which parents are willing to advocate for their children, making, for example, their concerns about academics known to teachers, is a critical factor in determining school success. Here one of our students concurs with the view that parental advocacy is critical because of the message it sends to the teacher:

The parents should go to all of the meetings of the parent-teacher organization [and go to] school one afternoon each month. Because you help your son's or daughter's progress in class. If you help the teacher, the teacher help your children.

In practice, this means giving students space to evaluate school expectations rather than prescribing conformity to school norms. In one of our classes, for example, a student brought in a flyer from her daughter's school with a list of ways parents can help their children with homework. Rather than going over the list point by point and discussing what parents should do to help their kids, as a teacher in a transmission classroom might have, the teacher, Loren McGrail, did something quite different. After reading the flyer, she posed questions such as, "Which of these things do you already do? Which would you like to do? Which do you think are ridiculous, impossible, or not useful? What do you already do that's not listed on the flyer?" This way of framing the reading led to a discussion of cultural differences in perceptions of teachers' versus parents' roles; parents identified both their own strengths and new things they might like to try. By relating the flyer to their own realities, looking at it in a broader social context, and exploring new possibilities, they maintained a stance of independence in the learning process. The flyer became the basis for shaping some of their own choices.

Program implication:

Parents should be encouraged to evaluate their children's schooling critically, rather than to give unquestioning support. The family literacy classroom should be a safe context for exploring attitudes and concerns about education as well as developing advocacy skills where necessary.

Finally, the prevalent focus among educators on parents' inadequacies obscures examination of social conditions that give rise to literacy problems. When issues like overcrowded housing, parents' need to have two jobs, and child care problems are seen as external obstacles, separate from and interfering with learning, literacy itself can become one more burden. When, on the other hand, these issues are fully integrated into the content of learning, so that analysis and action on them are central to the curriculum, literacy can become significant in learners' lives (Ada, 1987; Collier, 1986; Díaz, Moll, & Mehan, 1986). The following two examples from the same student's work show the difference between an approach that sees the social context as an external impediment to learning, and one that incorporates it into curriculum content (Auerbach, 1989).

Why I didn't do the Homework

Because 1). the phone is ringing

2). the door is noking

3). the kid is yumping

4). the food is burning

5). time runs fast

(p. 165)

At Home

I talk to my kids about school

I ask...¿Cómo se portaron?

They say very good.

I continue in ask

about the food...and the homework.

They speak to me in English....

I say I am sorry....

Yo no entendí nada; por favor háblame

en español....The older boy say OK...OK

You study english you are supposed to

understand. They repeat again to me

Slowly and more clearly. Yo les digo...

Muchas gracias.... I love you.

They are 4, 6, and 10 years old.

(p. 179)

When the student wrote the first piece, she was in a fairly traditional grammar-based classroom; the teacher had assigned some homework exercises that none of the students had done. This piece of writing was a response to the teacher's exasperated request for an explanation. The student was saying that the type of literacy work assigned was in conflict with the demands of daily living. In the second case, the student was in a family literacy class where the teacher had invited students to investigate and write about some of the dynamics of language choice in the home. In this case, the content revolved around exactly the issues that the student was concerned about in her daily life. Literacy was no longer in opposition to the student's concerns but rather a tool for reflecting and acting on those concerns.

Program implication:

Contextual factors and social conditions that shape learning should be incorporated into the content of literacy instruction through a participatory process allowing students to use literacy as a tool to address those conditions.

Alternative Models: A Participatory Approach

Our findings in the UMass Family Literacy Project suggest an approach that stands the transmission-of-school-practices model on its head: Rather than school practices and expectations informing family literacy instruction, parental practices and concerns must inform literacy education. Learners must be involved in researching the issues and literacy uses in their own lives. In order to do this, the notion of a predetermined curriculum must be discarded in favor of a participatory process that involves learners in curriculum development at every step of the way, from determining content to evaluating learning. The process entails the following key steps:

1. Investigating and identifying critical issues, literacy strengths, and needs in participants' lives. Students must participate in this process both inside and outside the classroom.

2. Developing curriculum content based on these student issues through participatory classroom activities, such as problem posing, language experience stories, dialogue journals, picture and photo stories, sociodramas, and written and oral histories.

3. Extending literacy outside the classroom, in families, communities, and schools through activities and actions that address student issues.

By inviting participants to bring their social context into the classroom, the process moves from the students to the curriculum rather than from the curriculum to the students. As literacy is used to address participants' concerns, it may become socially significant for family and community life.

Several publications describe in detail our approach to curriculum development, including guidelines for participatory curriculum development and examples from practice (Auerbach, 1989, 1992; Auerbach & McGrail, 1991; Nash, Cason, Rhum, McGrail, & Gomez-Sanford, 1992). One final example is included here to illustrate the development of the process. At one point, several of the project teachers noted that there seemed to be tension about the dynamics of family interactions around homework. We decided as a group to investigate this further, using the following teacher-generated dialogue (Nash et al., 1992) to trigger discussion in several different classes:

Father: Do you have homework today?

Linda: Yes, but I need help. The teacher told us to ask parents for help.

Father: Hmmm, let's see.

Linda: What does that say, Daddy?

Father: Hmmm, The...little...girl?

Linda: What's the matter, Dad?

Father: Don't rush me! (p. 35)

Although each of the classes used the same dialogue, the issues that emerged were different for every group. In one class, students focused on being tired and having too much housework as factors interfering with helping children with homework. In another, the focus was more on issues of communication with the school and understanding report cards. In a third, parents talked about having to hide their literacy problems from their children to maintain respect and, at the same time, devising ways of helping their children even if they themselves could not read the assignment. Each of the classes developed responses to the tensions presented in the dialogue that corresponded to their analysis of the issues, from sharing household responsibilities to ways of helping their children with homework despite reading problems. If the teachers had begun the discussions with a predetermined list of guidelines for working with children, rather than letting the adults relate to the text in their own ways, they may have missed the underlying issues and silenced students. Instead, by posing a problem with no prescribed solutions, each class unearthed very different contextual factors and followed its own path in addressing concerns.

Conclusion

The kinds of questions that have been raised in this chapter—questions about who uses literacy, in what language, and for what purposes, how literacy shapes family life, and how home and school practices interact with each other—are precisely the issues that we should be addressing with students inside the classroom. It is this process of collaborative investigation, critical analysis, and negotiation that will pave the way for parents to become active participants in their own and their children's education, ultimately leading toward the kinds of involvement that will improve not only our school systems, but, more importantly, our students' lives.

References

Ada, A.F. (1987). The Pajaro Valley experience: Working with Spanish-speaking parents to develop children's reading and writing skills in the home through the use of children's literature. In T. Skutnabb-Kangas & J. Cummins (Eds.), *Minority education: From shame to struggle* (pp. 223-238). Clevedon, England: Multilingual Matters.

Auerbach, E.R. (1989). Toward a social-contextual approach to family literacy. *Harvard Educational Review, 59*(2), 165-181.

Auerbach, E.R. (1992). *Making meaning, making change: Participatory curriculum development for adult ESL literacy.* Washington, DC and McHenry, IL: Center for Applied Linguistics and Delta Systems.

Auerbach, E.R., & McGrail, L. (1991). Rosa's challenge: Connecting classroom and community contexts. In S. Benesch (Ed.), *ESL in America: Myths and possibilities* (pp. 96-111). Portsmouth, NH: Boynton/Cook.

Collier, V.P. (1986). Cross-cultural policy issues in minority and majority parent involvement. In *Issues of parent involvement and literacy* (pp. 73-78). Washington, DC: Trinity College, Department of Education and Counseling.

Cummins, J. (1981). The role of primary language development in promoting educational success for language minority students. In *Schooling and language minority students: A theoretical framework* (pp. 3-49). Sacramento: California Department of Education.

Davies, D. (1980). An afterword: Co-production as a model for home-school cooperation. In R. Sinclair (Ed.), *A two-way street: Home-school cooperation in curriculum decision making* (pp. 69-76). Boston: Institute for Responsive Education.

Delgado-Gaitan, C. (1987). Mexican adult literacy: New directions for immigrants. In S.R. Goldman & K. Trueba (Eds.), *Becoming literate in English as a second language* (pp. 9-32). Norwood, NJ: Ablex.

Díaz, S., Moll, L., & Mehan, K. (1986). Socio-cultural resources in instruction: A context specific approach. In *Beyond language: Social and cultural factors in schooling language minority children* (pp. 187-230). Los Angeles: California State University.

Heath, S.B. (1983). *Ways with words.* Cambridge: Cambridge University Press.

McKay, S., & Weinstein-Shr, G. (1993). English literacy in the United States: National policies, personal consequences: *TESOL Quarterly. Vol. 27* (3), 399-419.

Nash, A., Cason, A., Rhum, M., McGrail, L., & Gomez-Sanford, R. (1992). *Talking shop: A curriculum sourcebook for participatory adult ESL.* Washington, DC and McHenry, IL: Center for Applied Linguistics and Center for Applied Linguistics.

Snow, C. (1987). Factors influencing vocabulary and reading achievement in low income children. In R. Apple (Ed.), *Toegepaste Taalwetenschap in Artikelen Special 2* (pp. 124-128). Amsterdam: ANELA.

Taylor, D. (1983). *Family literacy: Young children learning to read and write.* Exeter, NH: Heinemann.

Taylor, D., & Dorsey-Gaines, C. (1988). *Growing up literate: Learning from inner city families.* Portsmouth, NH: Heinemann.

Urzúa, C. (1986). A children's story. In P. Rigg & D. S. Enright (Eds.), *Children and ESL: Integrating perspectives* (pp. 93-112). Washington, DC: Teachers of English to Speakers of Other Languages.

Wells, G. (1986). *The meaning makers: Children learning language and using language to learn.* Portsmouth, NH: Heinemann.

CHAPTER 6
Memories of Mami
in the Family Literary Class

Loren McGrail

Each time I glance at the cover of *Memories of Mami, Writings from the Family Literary Project*, the use of the word *literary* instead of *literacy* makes me smile. A slip of the pen? No, Piedad, the student who volunteered to make the cover, was reminding us, practitioners in family literacy, that writing is for real purposes and for real audiences, not just for developing literacy skills. *Memories of Mami* is the title of the second collection of writings from the English Family Literacy Project at El Centro Del Cardenal in Boston. The purpose was to commemorate Mother's Day, to pay homage to our mamis/mommies. The audience was other Spanish-speaking students studying English. The writings began as dialogue journal entries written the weekend before Mother's Day. They were so moving I asked the group if they would share them with each other. They not only agreed to share them but asked if we could photocopy them and make them into a book so others could read them, too. This is how the family literacy project became the family literary project, or one of the ways the participatory approach played itself out in my classroom.

The participatory approach is a process of curriculum development that involves students in determining the content, processes, and outcomes of the curriculum as it emerges. In this context, curriculum development is a negotiation process where teachers and students participate as co-learners or co-investigators to determine which social or cultural issues to turn into the focus of literacy activities. The curriculum emerges as the result of this ongoing collaborative investigation of critical themes. In a family literacy project or class, the hope is that by incorporating community cultural norms and social issues into the curriculum, the social significance of literacy in family life will be heightened, and parents will increase their literacy proficiency as well as become more active participants in their children's education.

The challenge is knowing how to do this, how to connect what happens outside the classroom to what happens inside it so that students can make significant social changes in their individual and family lives. In *Making Meaning, Making Change* (1992), Elsa Auerbach outlines four things an educator needs to implement a participatory approach:

A clear conceptualization of the rationale for the approach;

An overview of the process;

A set of tools and procedures for finding and developing student themes; and

A set of resources to draw on in implementing the approach, including materials and co-workers to talk about the process as it develops. (p. 42)

In this chapter, I discuss how writing can be used to find and develop student issues and themes.

Writing is more than an exercise for improving literacy skills or even a vehicle for self-evaluation; it is a way students can contribute knowledge to the community both inside and outside the classroom. By writing thoughts and ideas down and working on a piece of writing over several drafts, students are able to recover, discuss, and revalidate their own history, cultural traditions, and values. Writing allows learners not only to reveal but also to discover their beliefs. In other words, they can use writing both to remember and to examine or to reconceptualize their life experiences. By making their writing public (publishing), learners also come to see writing as a way to establish a relationship with other adult learners who might not only be interested in their stories, but might even become inspired and write themselves, thus starting the composing cycle again. Publishing students' writing is a tool I used throughout the different phases of the participatory curriculum process.

As shown in Figure 1, the composing process, which consists of nonlinear and recursive phases (prewriting, drafting, revising, and editing), works well with the participatory curriculum process, which has four phases (Auerbach, 1992).

Figure 1.
Writing and Curriculum Development Processes

Steps in Writing Process	Curriculum Development Process
Getting started/prewriting • free writing • brainstorming • branching • problem trees • dialogue journals	*Listening To* *and* *Finding Themes*
Drafting/revising/editing • photostories • LEA stories • writing before and after readings • revising texts (including sharing and responding to texts) • editing	*Exploring Themes* *or* *Topics*
Publishing • letter writing • public readings	*Extending Literacy to Action Inside and Outside the Classroom*
Portfolios/writing folders • process and progress checklists • learning logs	*Evaluating Learning and Actions*

For *listening to* and *finding themes,* free writing, brainstorming, branching, problem trees, and dialogue journals work well in scratching the surface of issues. For *exploring themes or topics,* photostories, language experience (LEA) stories, writing before and after readings, and drafting, revising, responding to, and editing texts help learners to dig deeper. Letter writing, public readings, and publishing are successful in *extending literacy to action inside and outside the classroom.* Finally, for *evaluating learning and actions,* writing folders or portfolios of all writings, process and progress checklists, and learning logs are helpful ways for learners and teachers to assess change over time.

The following are examples and discussion of what some of these activities and processes looked like in my classroom of 12 Spanish-speaking women. Our publishing project, "Mothers are Teachers," illustrates how the four phases of the participatory process mirror the composing process.

Some of the activities fit neatly into their assigned phase while others cross boundaries. A good example of this boundary crossing is dialogue journals. I have used them, as have others before me (see Peyton & Staton, 1991), as a way to let students talk on paper. As such, they are a rich source of generative themes and good places to find issues to develop into literacy activities (see McGrail, 1991). However, due to the nature of the dialogue itself, which is initiated by prompts or questions from a teacher or peer, they can also be a way for an individual student to explore an issue in depth.

Listening to and Finding Themes

The following dialogue journal entry was written by a mother who often wrote about her children. It concerns a topic that is of utmost concern to mothers who have to put their children in day care so they can attend school or go to work.

Day Care

I have a big problem because my daughter doesn't like her Day Care. She is 3 years old. Why doesn't she like it? I think these are children in the classroom. She also doesn't like the food and the milk is too cold. My daughter likes warm milk. There are different teachers. My daughter doesn't like all the teachers. Now I wait because the people say give it time maybe one month and she will like it. I hope so because I'm very sad when I see my daughter because the life in the U.S. is too expensive and I must study English to get better work.

My response and her following entry reveal the give and take of information and concern regarding issues of real importance to the learners that took place in our class. The learner was being heard.

Hilda—I was talking to a friend of mine who is a mother with a 3 yr. old and she said that between the ages of 2 and 4 that some children experience "separation anxiety" or "fear of strangers" very strongly. Your daughter may be going through this. Why do you like the teacher? Why doesn't she like her? Did she tell you? Can you talk with the teacher? Does she speak Spanish? Can you tell her how you feel?

Her response to me:

Teacher you right because now my daughter she feel good, I think because she has many friends and she played four other children. Now I'm happy, but I have precaution with my daughter because I know everybody have to (be) careful when you have baby in one day care.

The following entry shows another familiar topic for my students: what language they speak, to whom, and when. (See McGrail, 1991, for an in-depth look at how this theme was developed into a cycle of literacy activities.)

I don't feel good when the people in the street speak to me in English because I understand everything but I can't speak good English. My son and my daughter speak only English but they speak to me in Spanish. When I speak on the telephone with my doctor or my social worker I speak English but not good English but they understand me. Maybe in future I can speak English with everybody.

(Carmen M.)

Exploring Themes or Topics

The following texts come from learners' writings after they had read some stories with their children. We were exploring the use of bilingual books for reading with children. We had a collection of about 12 books. Some had English and Spanish on the same page, others were translated from English to Spanish. The assignment was to choose one or two and take them home and read with their children. I did not say who should read or in what language. The goal was for them to do what felt comfortable and then answer a questionnaire that we would then use to explore the issues or concerns that came up for them as they did this reading.

The second part of the assignment was to write on a piece of paper anything they wanted about what happened during the reading together. The questionnaire and the writings told me many things about how my students viewed the reading process for themselves and for the children. For example, Flory's words, "I had to read the same book 3 or 4 time for I hors," represent an important insight that prompted much discussion about why children like to hear the same story over and over again at a certain stage of development. It also made us question whether this was true for ourselves as well.

When I went to the laibrery to bring two book for my child I read the book El Gato Galano My children interest in very much because it in Spanish I had to read the same book 3 o 4 times for 1 hors. I like to read always to my kids.

Margarita's retelling of the story, *The Stolen Apples,* includes a vocabulary list she started for herself, which illustrates the dual nature of the learning that occurs when parents read with their children. Parents can improve their own literacy while helping their children improve theirs.

The Stolen Apples

The horse had an apple tree and one day the apples were gone. Then he started to look for them and he found them the and them in there mouth.

I read the book to my son.

The interesting party is when he gives every one apples and still had two for the bear and him. Waoh! Thats a good story he said.

Vocabularie

| growled | maullar | |
| sudden | pronto | soon |

Finally, Angela's comment in her dialogue journal about the following passage from the bilingual feminist book, *My Mother the Mail Carrier* (Maury, 1976), shows not only that she comprehended the text, but also that she related it to her own life and her relationship with her daughter. She explored this relationship with great compassion throughout her journals and in her published writings. Both English and Spanish versions of the text are shown here, as they are in the book.

My mother is a good cook

I helped my mother make tamales when her new friend Pablo came to dinner. He said they were great, as good as his mother's, almost. My mother's face turned pink. He told us his mother became a very good cook after she stopped singing and stayed home. "That was wrong," my mother said. "She should have gone on singing." "No," said Pablo, "that was right. A woman's place is in the home." Nobody said much after that, and as soon as he finished the custard dessert, he left.

My mother was so mad that she started to cry, but then I jumped on her lap and sang all of "Sana, sana!" to her.

Mi mamá es buena cocinera

Yo ayudé a mi mamá a hacer tamales cuando vino Pablo, un compañero de trabajo, a cenar. Él nos dijo que estaban sabrosísimos, casi tan ricos como los que hacía su mamá. Las mejillas de mi mamá se pusieron bien rosaditas. Nos dijo Pablo que su mamá, después que dejó de trabajar como cantante, se dedicó al cuidado de su casa y llegó a ser muy buena cocinera.

—Hizo mal,—dijo mamá,—debía seguir con el canto.

—No,—dijo Pablo,—hizo bien. Una mujer debe dedicarse a su hogar.

Nadie habló mucho después de eso, y tan pronto como terminó de comerse el flan, se fue.

Mi mamá estaba tan enojada que se puso a llorar, pero entonces me senté en su regazo y le canté "¡Sana, sana!" a ella.

(From *My Mother the Mail Carrier*, by Inez Maury. Published by the Feminist Press at The City University of New York. All rights reserved. Reprinted by permission.)

Dear Loren,

I was reading the story for my is very nice because her daughter feel good when her mother is singing. I can see between in mother and daughter good relation.The daughter helped her mother to cook, when her new friend came to dinner, he liked that dinner, and he said my mother after she stopped to sing is good cook. Pablo think the woman is for home and take care of children. The hers mother felt anger and her daughter singing the same verse sana, sana.

Your friend,
Angela

Extending Literacy to Action and Evaluating Learning and Actions

As mentioned previously, this group of learners was involved in drafting, revising, and publishing their own writing. The publishing project, "Mothers are Teachers," as it later became named, is a cycle of writing activities that illustrates how the four phases of the participatory process mirror the composing process. This project shows how the writing process approach and the participatory approach worked hand-in-hand to help learners find a theme of deep personal interest (prewriting), to explore it (drafting), to share it with others (responding, revising, editing, and publishing), and to reflect on how it was developed (evaluating).

The writings that make up the typed and stapled booklet, "Mothers are Teachers," came into being by accident or, more accurately, spontaneously. The theme emerged from a card game I had created to investigate who teaches our children and what they teach them. I had two stacks of cards. The pink stack had words like *friend, brother, elementary school teacher.* The green stack had phrases like *learning to fix a meal, learning to read, learning to accept other people's differences.* I laid out all the phrase cards on a table to check learners' understanding of the vocabulary and idiomatic expressions. Then we drew one card at a time from the *people* cards and the learners matched the person with the appropriate learning activity or activities. We all took turns and explained our choices. When one of the students drew the card for *mother* we decided unanimously that mothers did all the activities. We all laughed. This is why we were so tired all the time. This prompted some women to tell stories about other learning activities they did with their children.

Though there was a lot of energy around this topic, I followed my original lesson plan, which was to ask the class to interview someone who had taught someone something. It was a good ethnographic exercise but totally inappropriate. The assignment should have been to go home and write about how you teach your children. Luckily for me, Angela had written in her journal how she had taught her daughter good habits. After the assignment was completed, I asked Angela to share her writing, to bring the class back to the topic they really wanted to write about. This is one of those rare moments when I had the good sense to listen to my students (a journal entry) and let them dictate what the content and direction of the class should be.

The next day almost everyone, including me, came in with a piece of writing. I asked people to share their writings with us by reading aloud or letting me or another classmate read. Sometimes we had several readings. The purpose of this read aloud was to let the author learn about her writing with her own mouth and ears. As Peter Elbow puts it, "With our mouths we feel how our words and phrases and sentences work. With our ears we hear how our words sound and also the words of others. What's nice is that this learning is physical, it occurs quickly without teaching" (Elbow & Belanoff, 1989, p. 3). After sharing our writing with no feedback allowed, either negative or positive, we then went around the circle and responded to the writings. We talked about what we understood (sayback), what we felt worked and why, and what we had questions about. Sometimes I modeled the process, and other times it just happened naturally.

A good example of how the group helped one author was the group's response to Blanca's story. Blanca had written about trying to teach her son how to tie shoelaces. It was a confusing piece, and none of us was clear why he couldn't learn this until someone asked her what kind of sneakers he had. We found out he had velcro sneakers. He didn't need to learn how to tie. Later when he got high tops that had laces and velcro he learned without any trouble. With this cleared up, Blanca was able to make her second draft much clearer. We as a group also learned through the metaphor of velcro sneakers that you can't learn something you're not interested in or don't need to know, another reminder to me of how important it is to stay tuned to learners' needs.

We had a writing workshop every day for 15 to 20 minutes. Sharing and responding to writing in this manner was ideally suited to my ESL class, where attendance was never consistent. During the author's circle or peer revising time, the only rule I insisted on was that we not focus on grammar corrections unless grammar problems blocked our understanding. This was both a relief and a difficult concept for my students to grasp, because they had internalized the belief that error correction was the legitimate way to respond to writing. Each time a student brought in a draft, we tried to follow this model of non-evaluative feedback. Some students tape recorded the peer revision group's discussion so they could play it again at home before working on their next draft. When learners felt their pieces were complete, we worked on grammar correction.

However, because I was new to process writing myself and not completely secure about only responding to and not correcting early drafts of writing, I experimented with grammar worksheets in my own written responses to students' first drafts. I dutifully looked for common mistakes and then either copied the sentences with the errors for them to correct or made multiple choice sentences in which they had to choose the grammatically correct sentence. Though the students really liked working on these grammar activities, it came too early in the process. They weren't ready to focus on grammar and mechanics; they wanted to change the content of what they were saying based on the questions and suggestions from the peer revising group. My grammar worksheet was a nice but useless activity at this stage of the process.

After reading the second drafts, I decided to take another approach. I wrote each student a note responding to the new draft in much the same way as we had done orally for the first draft. I also starred sentences that needed work and underlined misspelled words. When the students got their second drafts with these letters attached, they immediately shared them with each other. Again taking the lead from them and their desire to share these feedback letters, I encouraged them to work collaboratively to make whatever changes they felt necessary. During this time I also showed them some published booklets of student writings from previous classes and asked them if they wanted to publish their own. They all said enthusiastically that they did. This helped motivate them to work on yet another draft. However, with publication came a renewed concern for producing error-free writing. As students started to complete their third drafts, I asked them if they wanted to take pictures of their children to go along with their writings. For some of the more reluctant writers, this was further inspiration to write a book with pictures.

The last phase of the writing process was collecting all the students' many drafts, stapling them together, and giving them to everyone so that we could all rejoice in each other's progress from first draft to final copy. Angela's first and final drafts are shown here.

Mother's teacher

I taught of mi daughter to eat when she was bebe and to play. Go to the bathroom, looking for her clothes. When my daughter was 5 year I taught she had go to school. Now, she is 7 years old she to know to order all cloth shoes and her toy Now she know different thing but sometime forgive all. I think is natural because she is a little girl and she doesn't have all responsibility I alway tried taught good habit for better life for her

Mother's Teachers

I taught my daughter to eat by herself, when she was baby. I also taught her how to play, to use the toilet, to find her clothes and put them on.

When my daughter was 5 years old, she told me—"Mom, I want to go to school. I send her to private school for several months. Soon we came to live in Boston. Here se went to school.

Now she is 7 years old. Everyday I help her made the homework, and to look for something. Sometimes—she is lazy and she said "Mom help me tie my shoes." When I don't have time I said "I can't." She said, "Yes, you can because you are my mother and all mothers help their children."

Now she likes to go to School and share with me her class. I want my daughter to learn good habits for a better life.

This reflection of our individual and collective processes was as important as the book we published, for it provided written proof that the women were learning English. We also learned that, yes, we mothers are teachers, not just for our children, but for each other as well. Blanca, one of the students, captured this spirit in the following piece.

...sometimes when I saw some pictures, I remembered things, I had experienced in the past.

Other pictures I saw took me places I had never been and gave me knew experiences.

My teacher and classmates shared a lot. I feel we have a family with us.

Conclusion

Literacy research has shown us, and my students have taught me, that writing along with reading is a meaning-making process, a form of social action. It is a tool that validates practical subjective knowledge that people create by interacting with others. This subjective knowledge becomes critical knowledge as it moves through the phases of self-reflection and dialogue, the touchstones of participatory pedagogy and practice. In an atmosphere of trust, community, and creative process, parents in my class asserted their right to be heard and read. They asserted their right to make history and create literature, a world they can share with their children

References

Auerbach, E.R. (1992). *Making meaning, making change: Participatory curriculum development for adult ESL literacy.* Washington, DC and McHenry, IL: Center for Applied Linguistics and Delta Systems.

Elbow, P., & Belanoff, P. (1989). *Sharing and responding.* New York: Random House.

Maury, I. (1976). *My mother the mail carrier.* New York: Feminist Press.

McGrail, L. (1991). Full cycle: From journal writing to "codes" to writing. In J.K. Peyton & J. Staton (Eds.), *Writing our lives: Reflections on dialogue journal writing with adults learning English* (pp. 60-64). Englewood Cliffs, NJ: Regents Prentice Hall and Center for Applied Linguistics.

Peyton, J.K., & Staton, J. (Eds.). (1991). *Writing our lives: Reflections on dialogue journal writing with adults learning English.* Englewood Cliffs, NJ: Regents Prentice Hall and Center for Applied Linguistics.

CHAPTER 7
Literacy From Within: The Project FIEL Curriculum

Ana Huerta-Macías

...tiene uno como padre que aprender y mucho que enseñarle uno a sus hijos. (As a parent one has much to learn and much to teach one's children.)

(Parent participant, Project FIEL)

Estoy consiente que para poder enseñar a mis hijos bien, primero tengo que aprender yo. (I realize that in order to teach my children I first have to learn.)

(Parent participant, Project FIEL)

Early childhood educators and child developmentalists stress attention to the development of the whole child—cognitive, emotional, social, and physical. Yet, first-grade children, adolescents, and adults are often expected to learn through a regimen of teacher-centered, isolated skill exercises. These exercises often have no relation to the students' needs, background strengths, or passions and hopes. We at Project FIEL agree with respected researchers and practitioners (Edelsky, 1990; Harste, Woodward, & Burke, 1984; Rigg & Enright, 1986) who point out that a developmental, holistic approach giving emphasis to social context is dramatically important in all learning and especially in the areas of language and literacy development. Furthermore, we emphasize that it is a benefit to acknowledge and use as a point of departure the following facts:

- Children develop in dynamic interaction with other developing children and adults.

- Children from linguistically and culturally diverse backgrounds are developing within the context of constant interactions between home and school cultures.

Project FIEL

Project FIEL, Family Initiative for English Literacy, was a comprehensive program designed to provide participatory literacy and biliteracy development for limited-English-speaking families. The program offered a bilingual setting where parents and children worked together using a five-step instructional model that relied heavily on their prior knowledge and sociocultural strengths.

In 1985, a needs assessment conducted by the Literacy Center of El Paso Community College indicated that the most pressing reasons adults wanted to learn to read were to help their children with their homework and to read to them. In response to this need, an intergenerational literacy pilot project was developed, funded by the Texas Education Agency. The success of this project led to Project FIEL, a bilingual program funded by a three-year federal grant from the Office of Bilingual Education and Minority Languages Affairs (OBLEMA). Project FIEL was implemented from 1988-1991 by the Literacy Center in seven school districts in the El Paso area.

Project FIEL had four major goals:

1. To enhance the literacy and biliteracy development of the parents and children through a series of participatory intergenerational activities.
2. To provide information to the parents regarding the literacy development of their children, and to provide a setting for the parents to use the information.
3. To enhance parents' self-confidence to contribute to their children's literacy development through participatory group interaction.
4. To empower the parents to connect literacy activities to their own social and cultural situations, thus encouraging their use of literacy for personal, family, and community purposes.

In Project FIEL, parents attended class with their prekindergarten, kindergarten, or first-grade children once a week in small-group instruction. The curriculum emphasized role modeling, classroom participation, home activities, and cultural and linguistic reinforcement.

Theoretical Framework for Project FIEL

The three theoretical orientations that affected the original design and implementation of Project FIEL were Freire's (1973) critical pedagogy, parent involvement, and holistic learning. Critical pedagogy stresses participatory learning based on learners' past experiences and present learning and living needs. In the case of our family literacy population, the needs of the parents and children who were to be served by the project and the social context of strong family bonds dictated that we provide a setting where parents and children could work together.

The other two premises are solidly grounded in past research in the fields of literacy and language acquisition. The first premise was that parent involvement has a positive effect on children's lives (Careaga, 1988; Powell, 1990; Simich-Dudgeon, 1987). Parents in Project FIEL participated in class with their children and were encouraged to participate in their children's learning at home and in the community. The second premise was the importance of a holistic approach to learning, which emphasizes that language and literacy be taught naturally as they occur within a social environment (Auerbach, 1992; Goodman, 1986; Harste, Woodward, & Burke, 1984; Rigg & Enright, 1986). The use of code-switching was accepted as part of the holistic approach, which values the bilingual person's past sociocultural and sociolinguistic experiences and strengths (Edelsky, 1990). Past research on code-switching, which reveals it to be an effective teaching and learning strategy in bilingual contexts (Aguirre, 1988; Hudelson, 1983; Jacobson, 1990), further supported our acceptance of code-switching in the literacy classes.

FIEL Curriculum

The FIEL curriculum consisted of a series of lessons written by the staff with input from the participating parents and children. The choice of curriculum lessons was unique to each site. The themes for the lessons were selected through an initial program meeting and ongoing discussions with the participating families, in which they indicated their interests in particular themes offered to them and suggested the development of additional themes that they had a need for or interest in. Thus, the themes were learner-centered in the following ways:

- They had value for the participants.
- They used the participants' cultural and linguistic backgrounds as a point of departure.
- They were interesting to both parents and young children.
- They provided information for discussions in class and at home of issues significant to participants' lives.

These were some of the themes selected:
- Families (extended, single-parent, and so on)
- Food (family meal schedules, recipes, health versus junk food)
- Plants (including those native to the area)
- Music (Mexican and American)
- Heroes (personal, cultural)
- Cotton (cotton fields surrounded two of our schools)
- Books and You (families made their own books).

These themes were addressed through a flexible, five-step instructional model:

Step 1. Initial Inquiry: An oral language activity that encourages group interaction.

Step 2. Learning Activity: A concrete, hands-on activity done in family teams.

Step 3. Language Experience Approach Activity: A writing activity done in family teams.

Step 4. Storybook Demonstration: Storytime that encourages interaction.

Step 5. Home Activity Suggestion: Activities for the whole family to do at home.

The curriculum grew out of current beliefs about effective and ethical ways to encourage literacy. Freire and Macedo (1987) write that "the command of reading and writing is achieved beginning with words and themes meaningful to the common experience of those becoming literate, not with words and themes linked only to the experience of the educator" (p. 42). Similarly, Auerbach (1989) notes that if educators "define family literacy more broadly to include a range of activities and practices that are integrated into the fabric of daily life, the social context becomes a rich resource that can inform rather than impede learning" (p. 166). The way that social context and the background knowledge of parents and children can be used as a resource to promote literacy development is illustrated by a brief description of the curriculum surrounding some of the themes.

Lesson: Plants

The theme of plants, their use, their beauty, and how to cultivate them was chosen by participants in several of the sites. The following describes how the theme was developed in one of the rural sites. The discussion in Step 1., Initial Inquiry, began with families talking about their favorite plants. The conversation moved to the care of certain plants such as poinsettias, which one participant explained had to be kept in the dark for a certain amount of time before they could blossom. Plants common to the area were also described. This evolved into a long discussion of the medicinal use of plants. The parents were very knowledgeable about this and were eager to share their herbal remedies for headaches, stomach aches, upset stomachs, insomnia, burns, rashes, and even the use of herbs for dieting. The children, who were familiar with some of these remedies, occasionally chimed in to acknowledge their familiarity with a certain tea or to confirm that their stomach ache had indeed been cured with *istafiate* (an herb). By the end of the class, the parents walked away still sharing remedies while the children eagerly discussed what types of seeds they were going to plant for their home activity. As it turned out in this particular class, most of them planted beans, a staple in many of their diets. Thus, this aspect of the class also related to something that was common in the families' everyday experience.

Lesson: Cotton

As cotton fields surrounded two of our schools, it was natural that this topic be selected as a class theme at those sites. Again, a description of the implementation of this lesson in one of the classrooms serves as an example of how the curriculum built on the strengths and knowledge of the families.

It was clear from the discussion in Step 1 that several of the families, particularly the parents, were quite knowledgeable about the process of growing cotton. The parents carried most of the discussion during this phase, explaining the different stages of growth of the plant, the colors in the blossom, the time for picking, and the places where most of the cotton from the area was sent. It was apparent that the families felt confident and enthusiastic about sharing information with others in the class, particularly the instructor and staff, who did not know as much about cotton as they did. At one point a parent, Ms. R., corrected the instructor about the color of the blossom at one stage of the growth of the cotton plant:

Teacher: *Sale una flor amarilla...despúes se seca la flor.* (A yellow flower blooms...then it dries.)

Ms. R.: *No, se hace verde.* (No, it turns green.)

Teacher: *Se hace verde?* (It turns green?)

Ms. R.: *Sí, sí...se va abriendo y luego se seca.* (Yes, yes...it blossoms, then it dries.)

During this same lesson, Ms. R. expanded on the subject by talking about the difference between river and well water for growing cotton and fruits, again showing her expertise in this area:

Teacher: *Para el algodón se necesita un clima muy caliente y tropical, no sé aquí cómo crece....*(For cotton you need a very hot and tropical climate, I don't know how it is that it grows here....)

Adult 1: *Lo riegan mucho.* (They water it a lot.)

Adult 2: *También dicen que el mejor es del valle de Juarez.* (They also say that the best is from the valley in Juarez.)

Ms. R.: *De aquel lado...el agua del río no está buena, no está dulce...y el agua buena que teníamos allá sí era de pozo...no estaba sucia...con el agua del pozo salen las sandías dulces, la fruta....*(from that side...the river water is not good, it's not sweet...and the good water that we used to have over there [their former residence] was well water...it wasn't dirty...watermelons, fruit come out sweet with well water....)

Memories of years past when some of the families had worked in the cotton fields were also shared. One of the children, for example, mentioned her memories of being terribly frightened one day when she was with her mother; while playing in the field, she saw a snake. Mother and daughter shared the incident with the rest of the class, the parent commenting how she had run and grabbed a machete and killed the snake.

In the next steps in the lesson, the families shared information about the use of cotton in clothes and how little cotton is actually found in ready-to-wear garments these days. The children then volunteered to look at each of the tags on their shirts, sweaters, and jackets and excitedly shared the fiber content. Cotton plant collages with real cotton picked from nearby fields were later made. The class ended with a storybook about how cotton is processed and shipped to factories. Thus, the strength of the families, in this case their knowledge and experiences with cotton, were clearly drawn upon in the implementation of this class, which was meaningful, relevant, and personally interesting to the families.

Lesson: Books and You

This lesson was implemented at all sites and provided a great opportunity for parents and children alike to share their strengths and talents. A discussion of the families' favorite stories, poems, *dichos* (sayings), and *cuentos* (stories) took place in one of the classrooms. The families shared oral as well as written traditions. During Step 2, Learning Activity, when the class divided into family teams, each team made a book. Some family teams wrote and illustrated poems, some wrote about their families, some wrote about family traditions, while others illustrated or wrote about a variety of topics significant to their lives. The books, then, were a reflection of things significant to the lives of each of the families. As they shared their work with the others at the end of the class, it was obvious that the parents and children were in effect displaying their talents as they told their stories, recited their poems, or simply conveyed the importance of their illustrations to the group. An example of a story based on a family vacation written by a bilingual child follows:

memory trips

my 1° trip was to oklahoma city by car

my 2° trip was to mazatlan by airplane

my 3° trip was to acapulco by bus

my 4° trip was to mazatlan by airplane

my 5° trip was rocky point by truck

en el future va a ir a la luna el cohete

(In the future it will be to the moon by rocket)

Conclusion

Auerbach (1989) states,

Literacy is meaningful to students to the extent that it relates to daily realities....The teachers' role is to connect what happens inside the classroom to what happens outside so that literacy can become a meaningful tool for addressing the issues in students' lives. (p.166)

The FIEL curriculum provided this linkage between the classroom and the outside world by using the strengths of the families—their knowledge, experiential and other, their talents, their ability to reflect on their behaviors—to develop each of the themes in the lessons. Their sociocultural/linguistic past was validated as each of the themes was collectively molded by each particular group, with every group designing a unique tapestry of discussion, writing, and art activities, all of which enhanced their literacy development.

References

Aguirre, A. (1988). Code-switching, intuitive knowledge, and the bilingual classroom. In H.S. García & R.C. Chávez (Eds.), *Ethnolinguistic issues in education* (pp. 28-38). Lubbock, TX: Texas Tech University, College of Education.

Auerbach, E.R. (1989). Toward a socio-contextual approach to family literacy. *Harvard Education Review, 59*(2), 165-181.

Auerbach, E.R. (1992). *Making meaning, making change: Participatory curriculum development for adult ESL literacy.* Washington, DC and McHenry, IL: Center for Applied Linguistics and Delta Systems.

Careaga, R. (1988). *Keeping LEP students in school: Strategies for dropout prevention* (Program Information Guide No. 7). Rosslyn, VA: National Clearinghouse for Bilingual Education. (ERIC Document Reproduction Service No. ED 302 089)

Edelsky, C. (1990). Whose agenda is this anyway? A response to McKenna, Robinson, and Miller. *Educational Researcher, 19*(8), 7-11.

Freire, P. (1973). *Education for critical consciousness.* New York: Seabury.

Freire, P., & Macedo, D. (1987). *Reading the world and the word.* South Hadley, MA: Begin & Garvey.

Goodman, K. (1986). *What's whole in whole language?* Exeter, NH: Heinemann.

Harste, J.C., Woodward, V.A., & Burke, C.L. (1984). *Language stories and literacy lessons.* Portsmouth, NH: Heinemann.

Hudelson, S. (1983). Beto at the sugar table: Code-switching in a bilingual classroom. In T.H. Escobedo (Ed.), *Early childhood bilingual education: A Hispanic perspective* (pp. 31-49). New York: Teachers College Press.

Jacobson, R. (1990). Allocating two languages as a key feature of a bilingual methodology. In R. Jacobson & C. Faltis (Eds.), *Language distribution issues in bilingual schooling* (pp. 3-17). Philadelphia: Multilingual Matters.

Powell, D.R. (1990). *Families and early childhood programs.* Washington, DC: National Association for the Education of Young Children.

Rigg, P., & Enright, D.S. (1986). *Children and ESL: Integrating perspectives.* Washington, DC: Teachers of English to Speakers of Other Languages.

Simich-Dudgeon, C. (1987). Involving LEP parents as tutors in their children's education. *ERIC/CLL News Bulletin, 10*(2), 3-4.

CHAPTER 8

Our Stories to Transform Them: A Source of Authentic Literacy

Maritza Arrastía

"A story, like life, is a journey." This is how storyteller Mary Savage opened our first session in the spring of 1990. Our learning community of Latina, Chinese, and African-American women from the Lower East Side of New York City explored the richness of our individual and collective inner worlds through the vehicle of traditional and personal stories.[1]

The Mother's Reading Program, which began in January 1984, is predicated on a belief in the richness of the individual and shared inner worlds of our students. Further, we hold the conviction that this richness can be expressed through stories. The individual writings produced by our community literature approach have been the concrete products of this richness and attest to that larger grammar of the human mind whereby experience is structured into tales. We believe that everyone is well educated in her own story, and that by making written texts from our stories, our predominantly oral community attains literacy in a way that affirms and transforms our existing culture, rather than invalidating, repressing, or replacing it as often happens in traditional educational settings.

We had several goals in exploring and telling stories:

• To deepen our knowledge and understanding of oral tradition, one of the major resources of the cultures represented in our programs;

• To deepen understanding and communication among women from three cultures by gaining insights into commonalities and

---

[1] The storytelling project team consisted of Mary Savage, storyteller; Ana Betancourt and Dawn Want, teachers; Irene Sosa, videographer; and me, the teacher-director of the Mother's Reading Program.

idiosyncracies of our cultures, by affirming true differences, and by exploding divisive false differences;

• To deepen the richness of our ongoing group and individual writing;

• To create stories to share with our children; and

• To videotape the project for documentation and for creation of learning materials.

To carry out the project, we expanded our existing program, which consists of two ABE classes for Latina and African-American women and one ESL class for Chinese women. To our class schedule of three weekly three-hour sessions, we added an additional three-hour session on Friday mornings for 13 weeks. This was open to all currently enrolled ABE and ESL students. Twenty women from the ABE classes (mostly Latina women) and six Chinese women chose to participate. Although the Friday class was a separate event, we found that the project carried over into our regular classes as we reflected on the storytelling process, retold stories, wrote stories, and made books for our children with the stories we had discovered.

Our sessions followed a predictable format. Initially the teacher was the scribe, but the learners took over as writers and as scribes for others as they mastered the conventions of writing. We began by sharing one or more "seed stories," primarily a traditional story told by the storyteller. Seed stories were used to start a conversation or to set us off on our writing journey. Next we conducted group dialogue about the stories and broke into small groups to tell and sometimes write our own stories. We regrouped for a closing, sharing session in which we used oral retelling, choral reading, chants, and songs from the stories to foster group participation. It was in sharing sessions like these that we explored how a story could be told as a piece of fresh, juicy gossip or could become an artifact whose telling could be worked on, elaborated, and enriched through voice and movement. The women retold stories at home with children, family members, and friends, and mined these listeners for other stories to bring back to the group.

Our project has indeed been a journey—into each story, into the many stories generated through the seed stories, into each of our lives and each others' lives, and into the very process of how to share stories across languages and cultures.

Early Sessions: Setting Off on Our Journey

In our early sessions, the primary seed stories told by the storyteller were selected to build on generative themes we had discovered during the recent election of a class steering committee, and to acknowledge that the storytelling process we were undertaking was itself a mystery to us. Therefore, these first stories were about governance, judgements, and riddles in which the story represented the exploration of a dilemma to be resolved. The key seed stories used here were: "The Bird and his Family" (a Sufi tale), "Chaste or Not," "The King and the Groom," "David and Bathsheba," and "Solomon's Judgment."

The first step in our journey involved transforming how we listened. We spent a lot of time developing the ability to listen actively. We have become proficient when listening actively during a dialogue, when crafting our own group and individual stories, and when reading our own stories together, but this did not come easily.

It was our habit, when first listening to an unfamiliar story, to become passive and tune out. We placed our faces into masks of attention while our minds were wandering away. Thus, we discussed that listening to stories must be engaging and active; that, indeed, the story cannot exist without the listeners' involvement. Not only did the storyteller explicitly tell us this, but we saw this to be true because the stories themselves came alive. We discovered that stories themselves can be the mechanisms for transformation. A story, like life, is indeed a journey, a facsimile of life, a compression of life, an image, a mirror, a skeleton, a piece of life. Ultimately, a story is an agent of life that teaches, questions, directs, resolves, and transforms.

The transformation occurs because the story's journey explores a psychic map. We followed myth, symbol, and image to trace the hidden paths of our inner worlds. The queens, stepmothers, talking birds, magic animals, inner treasures of our stories, woven in and out of the storyteller's seed stories and our unconscious minds, allowed us to glimpse unrecognized or disowned components of ourselves.

For example, one participant addressed this theme in her evaluation of the project. (This and the other quotes from project participants in this chapter came from written evaluations at the end of the project.)

I learned storytelling is a good way to teach our children things about us when we were small. For me it's been a learning experience, not play. I learned that when one tells a story all those present pay attention. If the story is funny they laugh with you but if it's sad everybody gets sad. When I told my story I returned to being small again. Something inside of me changed, I couldn't say exactly what changed, I don't know, but something changed. Now I feel I could tell my children stories in a more relaxed way. They're stories like our lives, things that happen to us, mainly when we were small. When I tell them a story about when I was small it is like taking a trip to the place where the story took place and i become small, very little, and I feel like I felt then...at that time. When mary, the storyteller, came she said we would go on a journey. We took the journey with her. I went to the forest to kill the beautiful bird with the many colored feathers (multi) and blue eyes called the freedom bird. I also went across the river with the billy goats to eat fresh, green grass on the other side of the bridge. The storyteller took us with her. I went with her.

(Elsa C.)

Thus, the storytelling project was the vehicle that took us from our separate classrooms where we coexisted in our distinct worlds as Asian, Latina, and African-American women to explore our commonalities together in one classroom. As a group, we explored and retold stories from India, China, Africa, Haiti, and Puerto Rico. The stories were about judgment, challenge, and trickery of wise people and of foolish people. There were tall tales, humorous tales, riddles, and myths. These seed stories generated a wealth of stories from our own childhoods, stories we'd lived and stories we'd heard.

The first session was built primarily on the voice of the storyteller; by the second session, the voices of the women had emerged. A series of short stories were told by many Latina women. One milestone for us was when one of the women in the Chinese ESL class shared a long story in Chinese, which was later translated into English by the teacher. This in turn elicited response stories by the Latina women. Our multicultural dialogue had reached a new stage.

Middle Sessions: Listener Becomes Teller

In this phase of our work, we used the following seed stories: "The Sun Man," "Juan Bobo," "Mumbo Jumbo," and "One Minute Tales." After four sessions, the sharing process had become familiar. While the stories continued to take us to unknown territories, we were familiar with participatory listening practices that tellers can use to move the narrative and the listeners. At one point, two of the program teachers and four of the students attended a conference. For those who remained—students, storyteller, teacher, tutor— storytelling became a vehicle to maintain their sense of community and deepen it.

When the students who did not attend the conference told the returning group of the storytelling they had missed, they used voice, movement, and sound. As they told their stories, they shared both the outer and the inner tale. They were now both listeners and tellers. The tools of storytelling were becoming part of our ways of being with one another. As one participant explained,

We, as a group of women feel happy about ourselves. I feel good about myself. I never thought I could write a book or be a storyteller myself. I feel more confident since I wrote the book and told my story to the class. The stories are about what really happened in my childhood. They're real, just like the people. They're our lives, they tell about things we actually did. This was learning and it was fun. Listening to the stories the words travel through my head and make me think about my own life, like when my brother and I used to do a lot of things together. The one that really got to me was about the girl whose mother sent her to the store during a storm first and then sent her to wash the clothes. When I was back home, when I was home, I used to do a lot of washing. The storyteller pulls people together. She makes us all feel good we are sharing something together. She sat down on the floor in the center of our circle.

(Louise R.)

Last Sessions: Return

We were now empowered to return, to bring the stories home to tell. One image in the generative story, "The Freedom Bird," is an apt metaphor for this phase: The freedom bird is cut up, placed in a box, bound, and buried under many stones; yet each broken fragment comes to life as its own bird, and when the stones are removed, the birds fly free. So it was with our buried stories. The stories were also taken home to the children; the mothers' books were made for and with their children. The children participated in some of our storytelling sessions. The women's reports of their children's clamoring to hear and rehear the mother's stories demonstrated that our affirmation of our cultures contributed to the children's greater appreciation of these cultures. We began to think in terms of selecting among the many stories those we wanted to make into children's books, to perform, or to compile into reading texts. We began to discuss how we wanted to share our tales and how to use videotape to document the project and to create learning materials such as companion video/text reading resources.

The women prepared a storytelling performance for the spring festival sponsored by Mother's Reading Program's primary funding agency, the Community Development Agency (CDA) of the City of New York. We discussed what performing for others might mean and began to understand storytelling as a gift to others, similar to offering food to guests. The fruit of the CDA festival experience and our dialogues about performing were evident during our own closing session for the project, which was a storytelling festival in which 19 women told stories in a spirit of self-confidence and sharing. One participant commented on how she used her gift of story with her own children:

> Yes, these are our stories because they happened to us, in our lives, they are our experiences. This was definitely learning and in a way playing. I feel different. I shared the stories with my children and I felt very happy. At the same time the children learn and they feel good when they tell their friends. When I told my children my story they wanted to play with me right away. One said, "Mami, let's play like you used to when you were small. Mami, get real rice and beans so we

can all play mother." My daughter evelyn said, "I'll be the mother and you'll be my children." I had to get all the raw ingredients to play "cooking" with all my children in the house

(Enirse R.)

The Project Team's Process

For the project team of teachers, storyteller, and videographer, the process has also been a journey. We needed to learn more about each other and each other's cultures in order to guide the learners. We discovered that seed stories generated very different stories among the Chinese, Latina, and African-American women. Chinese women shared more traditional stories, whereas the Latina and African-American women shared more personal ones. We found that animal stories had tremendous cross-cultural resonance and were a bridge among cultures. Story themes for the first sessions were teacher-generated based on the group's recent experiences in shared-class governance. These themes created a dynamic from the group that propelled the following sessions and became self-generating themes. As one participant commented,

I have learned to engage the others in dialogue. The stories are very special because they are true. I have learned a lot, my mind is very different from when we started. I feel it has shifted, I can see the imagination of other people. My mind is open. I receive happiness when we tell the stories.

The Journey: The Stories Do Not End

The storytelling process does not end, just as it does not begin, rooted as it is in the group's story-filled, organic, and natural style of conversation. One of the Mothers' Reading Program's projects at the beginning of the following year was generating and writing childbirth stories (these included stories we had been told about our own births, stories of the births of our children, and stories of births we knew about of our family members, friends, and even strangers). Even those stories of the earliest moments of life were shaped by our families' own stories and myths.

Because each particular story does have a beginning, middle, and end, and a story is a small manageable bit of our life, a story can be a laboratory for transforming our larger life. In telling our stories, learning each others' stories, and finding the strength and value in our stories, we began to change the stories and our roles as protagonists.

Each story has an end, but that end is a point of departure for the next teller's story, for our own next story. The end of the storytelling project provided us with many points of departure for future journeys, many seed stories for future telling.

We continued to use this year's stories in the curriculum as reading texts and as seeds for more telling. We printed two of the illustrated stories, one by a Chinese woman and one by a Latina woman. The books were trilingual editions—Chinese, Spanish, and English. The process of sharing stories increased the connection among the Latina women, the Chinese women, and the African-American women as the foundation for more multicultural telling.

The tellings also uncovered for us the roots of our written traditions. We have found in the wealth of fantastic stories that have emerged a source of Latin American magic realism. Stories shared by the Chinese women are a bridge to published written works by Chinese authors we plan to explore in the future.

Although telling personal and traditional stories has always been a part of our group writing process, we have learned how to deepen and develop this telling. By validating our oral tradition, exploring the richness of our oral literature, and transforming it into written texts, we are achieving authentic literacy. Having uncovered the roots of our written traditions, we began during the following years to read the works of Latina and Chinese writers. The texts were used in the same way we had used our own images, stories, and writings, as tools to generate dialogue. Reading the texts chorally in small segments allowed all members of our classes, including beginning readers, to participate.

Working with our stories provides an inexhaustible source of learning material and is an invaluable tool for transforming those stories, so that we become the makers, shapers, and protagonists of our own life tales.

On Replication

The purpose of telling stories, and of telling the story of the storytelling project, is to get others to tell stories as well. Storytelling is, indeed, a journey, inherently unknowable and unpredictable, but our project's experience can serve as a map for other teachers. Seed stories need to be selected with care and attention to the particularities of the class. Audiotaping the sessions (and videotaping, if possible) provides the basis for developing future texts and for examining the process.

Be prepared for the unpredictable. The very women who told us they had no stories came up with many stories, but it was necessary, besides seeding the process with stories, to leave a space of silence for the stories to emerge. It is important to have a repertoire of possible seed stories in case the silence takes longer than you foresee and because the telling can veer in many directions.

The following observation from one woman sums up the feelings of many of us who participated in this project.

The stories that we do in class teach us to tell stories to family, friends, anybody who wants to hear a story. We learned how to write a story and how to make a book out of a story. We learned to listen to the person telling the story. When mary came to the class to teach us how to listen to a story and how to tell a story it made a change. We were changed, I changed. It makes me understand what I read in the stories. I start to think about different things, our lives today and our lives in the past. I feel different now from before because i could write a story and understand stories better. These are our lives, our stories, when we were little girls. We did those things. Now that i've made a book that tells my story it makes me think about when I was a little girl playing outside with my goat. It brings back so many memories to me. It makes me think of happy times when I was little and the things that I did when I was little. The storyteller makes the stories very interesting to listen to.

(Vernia Mae F.)

Where We Are, Where We're Going

The first two sections of this book focus on issues of program design and curriculum development, drawing on existing programs and models for inspiration and example. In this section, issues of our broader vision are addressed. What are our ultimate purposes? How do we proceed based on those purposes? How will we know we are moving in the right direction? The chapters in this section articulate some of the challenges we face, but they also point out some of the potential rewards to those challenges.

In "Learning from Uprooted Families," I argue that in our work with families in multilingual communities we must learn about those we wish to serve. Part of what is needed is to learn and document how learners currently use literacy in their lives and how they wish to use it. I argue that part of our task is to invite learners to examine their own language and literacy use both outside the classroom and within our programs as part of the educational process. By making explicit what *is*, programs can help learners imagine what *could be*. The chapter ends with a set of queries for discussion and investigation by teachers and program planners, with the assistance of community leaders and multilingual families themselves.

In "Evidence of Success," Heide Spruck Wrigley confirms what we already knew from our work with learners: The reality of what they are learning and what we are doing is much messier than the neat numbers delivered by standardized tests. She challenges us to find ways to document that reality systematically and to create ways of comparing our experiences with those of others. This is crucial not only for the sake of our funders, but for ourselves to inform our own program planning, for teachers who must make a hundred decisions before and during every class lesson, and for learners who want to have a sense of their own progress.

Wrigley reminds us that assessment and evaluation do not have to be threatening. Just as learners need opportunities to examine their goals for literacy and to reexamine them as they gain new appreciation for the possibilities that literacy opens for them, we, too, need opportunities to reflect with colleagues on the purpose and meaning of our literacy work. Incorporating into our programs tools for ongoing assessment and evaluation of our efforts can be part of the challenging, but very gratifying, process of examining our vision with others, and seeing how that vision has changed and grown with our own experiences.

In "Magic and Risk: Lessons for the Future," Elizabeth Quintero reminds us that we are pioneers. Family literacy practitioners do not take the easy or the safe route. Working with those who do not share our agendas and listening to voices that we are not accustomed to hearing are risky endeavors as our own ways of knowing are no longer the ultimate authority. Yet, as Quintero argues, and as others in this volume bear witness, for those who are willing to take the risk, the rewards can be mighty for children, for adults, and for practitioners, all of whom are learning in synergy.

With deliberate investigation of literacy and its uses, with new partnerships that help us understand other ways of seeing, and with recognition of the strengths that multilingual families bring to their lives in a new setting, it becomes possible to imagine schools that understand and respond to families and communities, families that cooperate with schools toward agreed-on goals, and generations who find in one another the resources to remember their past and to take on the present and future with confidence and joy.

CHAPTER 9
Learning from Uprooted Families

Gail Weinstein-Shr

I feel so bad for these kids. The parents don't come to parent-teacher conferences. I've never seen any at open house either. I don't think they really try to help the kids with school. I wonder, maybe in their culture, education isn't as important.

(Third-grade teacher)

This teacher could be from anywhere in the United States. Like thousands of other teachers, she is concerned about the uprooted children in her classroom and would like to enlist their parents in supporting their school success. She can only guess at the scene "backstage," outside the classroom, where the action is usually quite invisible to her, and the players are not well understood.

The purpose of this chapter is to provide a glimpse behind the curtain, drawing primarily from the experiences of Southeast Asian refugees in the United States. The chapter begins with a brief discussion of the role of language and literacy in the lives of multilingual families. Next I discuss family literacy issues, urging that we expand our vision beyond the lens of the classroom to bring family and community life into view. Finally, I argue that in order to serve families as interdependent units, it is necessary to learn more about them not only in our planning and needs assessment, but also through the fabric of our daily work. The chapter ends with a set of queries

The first two sections of this chapter expand on a framework originally developed in "Literacy and Second Language Learners: A Family Agenda," in D. Spener (Ed.), (1994), *Adult Biliteracy in the United States*, Center for Applied Linguistics and Delta Systems.

I am grateful to the Spencer Small Grants program for support that made some of the research for this chapter possible. I also wish to thank Ilse Brunner for her thorough and thoughtful reading of a draft of this chapter.

for discussion and investigation by teachers and program planners, with the assistance of community leaders and multilingual families themselves.

Language, Literacy, and Everyday Lives

Refugee and immigrant adults are as diverse as the countries they come from and the circumstances that brought them here. Ethnic groups that may seem homogeneous can be extremely diverse in any number of ways. Linguistic diversity is one obvious way. Latin Americans, for example, may come from many different countries and may speak Spanish as a first or second language. Although Peruvians and Puerto Ricans may both speak Spanish as a native language, the varieties they speak may be so different as to impede mutual intelligibility. An indigenous Mayan from Guatemala may have learned Spanish as a lingua franca for the marketplace and may only speak it in a pidginized form. Filipinos, on the other hand, come from a tiny island where no less than 150 mutually unintelligible languages are spoken (California Department of Education [CDOE], 1986).

Second, rural/urban differences often accompany educational differences. For example, the first wave of Vietnamese, Cambodian, and Cuban refugees were university-educated city-dwellers, but later arrivals were farmers who had never held a pencil before seeking refuge. These groups bring with them very different experiences with formal schooling as well as with work, resulting in very dissimilar tools for adapting to life in the United States.

Religion is yet another source of difference; among Chinese, some are Christian, some are Buddhist, and others are avid atheists (CDOE, 1984). The differences go on. In a seemingly homogeneous Hmong refugee community in Philadelphia, for example, religious differences in degree of involvement with the Christian church reflect two subgroups with very different kinship patterns and different goals for literacy. One group is focused on assimilating into American society as quickly as possible, whereas the other group is most interested in using literacy to preserve tradition and to stay connected with the homeland (Weinstein-Shr, 1993). These kinds of differences have profound implications for planning educational programs, if our programs are to take into account the needs and resources of the families we serve.

Yet, despite the diversity among refugees and immigrants, similar themes repeatedly emerge as children and adults manage life in their new setting. The themes selected here grow from my own work with refugees in Philadelphia through Project LEIF.[2] These are survival, communication, and power, which are explored below.

Survival

Soldiers come we run always run. I have my baby inside. I run. Baby come out I can't rest. My family we hear guns. I run with baby. When we not run baby dead. Five my children die from Khmer Rouge in my country.

(Told to P. Lopatin, 1990)

Many refugees who have come to the United States are here despite all odds. Leaving their countries often meant surviving by physical endurance, sheer wits, and enormous emotional will. It is rare to find a Cambodian who has been spared the death of a family member by murder or starvation during flight. Hmong refugees moved large families through the jungles of Laos, walking with their children and infants by night, hiding in leaf-covered camps by day. The horrors encountered by Vietnamese "boat people" came to public attention with tales of family separation, loss at sea, brutal piracy, and hostile receptions on the other end of the nightmarish journeys. If refugees were indeed the helpless peasants that they are sometimes made out to be in the media, they wouldn't be here; they would be dead. Those who have made it to the United States are here because they are survivors.

The same survival resources that enabled people to escape under desperate conditions often serve them well as they adapt to life in a challenging new setting. One way of coping has been to draw on traditional kin resources. Hmong refugees of the same generation who share a clan name, for example, consider themselves brothers or sisters and expect to enjoy specific rights and fulfill expected obligations with their clan mates. In Laos, a man might be housed by a clan mate on a journey between villages; in the United States, one

---

[2] Project LEIF, Learning English through Intergenerational Friendship, is an intergenerational tutoring program in which college students tutor English to refugee elders. To date, more than 1,000 volunteers have worked with Hmong, Cambodian, Lao, Chinese, and Latino elders in Philadelphia. For more information, see Weinstein-Shr, 1989, and Lewis and Varbero, Chapter 3, this volume.

young Hmong leader reports that he can travel to a new city for a conference, look up his clan name in the phone book upon arrival at the airport, and expect to be picked up and housed by clan mates he has never met (Weinstein-Shr, 1993). This web of kin support can be a critical resource for some newcomers as they manage new lives in America.

A second way of managing in the face of trauma has been to draw on the traditional strengths of families while creating new kinds of families. Because of the unspeakable circumstances of flight, it is unusual for any Cambodian nuclear family, for example, to have resettled intact. As a result, Cambodian families in America are often reconstituted with survivors who create fictive bonds to cope with terrible loss (CDOE, 1988). Lao mothers who once formed cooperative groups for rearing children in Laos as an adaptive response to the loss of men in wars may continue these patterns of group support in America. These examples illustrate the remarkable adaptive resources of people under siege.

A third way of responding to a new setting is through the development of community organizations, such as Mutual Assistance Associations (MAAs), in which traditional forms of leadership may exist side by side with new ones. MAAs are a unique form of self-help in which members of the community organize to help themselves. Presidents of MAAs are often young men selected by the community to provide links with the English-speaking host culture. Yet the authority of these leaders is often shared or surpassed by elders whose influence in community matters is not as easily visible to monolingual Americans (see Lewis & Varbero, this volume). With traditional and new kinds of leadership in their communities, families may have a variety of resources available for solving a range of problems.

A fourth strategy for survival is to share resources and to find bargains that may not be visible to long-time residents. Hmong families in Philadelphia, for example, buy pigs wholesale at the outskirts of the city to butcher and share among family groups. Through informal networks, newcomers to a city may know of stores, unknown to local residents, where prices are negotiable. In addition, as with the nonliterate native speakers of English we learn about from Fingeret (1983), many refugees who have limited experience with print rely on social networks or their own wits to solve a wide variety of literacy-related problems (Weinstein-Shr, 1990). At Project

LEIF, when older adults were asked why they wanted to learn English, they rarely mentioned survival concerns (Weinstein-Shr & Lewis, 1991). Rather, most reported that they wanted to learn English to communicate with children or grandchildren. The second theme, then, is communication.

Communication

I love my grandchildren very much. I am learning English so I can talk to my grandchildren. But I also want them to understand a little Chinese. I think every language is useful!

(Susan Y.)

For uprooted families, resettlement in a setting where a different language is spoken profoundly affects newcomers' roles and relationships. The experiences of Project LEIF participants provide examples of these changes. One tutor recounted his change of perspective when he asked his quiet, serious, elder tutee a simple question: Were there open air markets in her homeland? Her grandson translated her answer, in which she told of how she would gather with women friends to eat and chat, spending many pleasant afternoons at the marketplace. Until then, the tutor had not imagined her as the bubbly, sociable, talkative person she must have been in her native setting. A Puerto Rican woman reported feeling like an outsider in her own children's homes when her grandchildren speak English and refuse to answer her in the language she understands. A Hmong woman spoke of her fear that her grandchildren will not know what life was like in Laos and that, as their linguistic repertoire changes, she will have no way to tell them.

Some uprooted groups make special efforts to promote oral and written native language development for cultural continuity. When bilingual programs are not provided by an American school district, some groups such as the Chinese pay to send their children to private Chinese weekend schools. Among some groups such as the Hmong, native language literacy has spread informally in some subcommunities.

Whereas certain uprooted groups create contexts for linguistic and cultural maintenance, other groups are anxious to acculturate as quickly as possible, and encourage their children to make the transition from the native language to spoken and written English. Some researchers suggest that language use among today's uprooted families may be affected more strongly by generation than by any other factor (McKay & Weinstein-Shr, 1993). This means that language plays an unprecedented role in the adaptation of families to their new lives and in their relationships to one another.

With more opportunities to hear, study, and interact in English, children learn the language of their new home much more quickly than their parents or grandparents do. As a result, adults must often rely on children for solving language-related and literacy-related problems. For parents of school-age children, this means relying on the children to decipher communications from school. One Cambodian man tearfully reported that his son had been expelled six months earlier. The boy left every morning at eight and returned at four, so the man did not know about the expulsion until six months later when a neighbor told him. He had, until then, depended on the boy to interpret messages from school. This raises the third theme that repeatedly emerges in the tales of newcomers: the theme of power and parental authority.

Power and authority

> *I have ears, but I am deaf! I have a tongue, but I am mute!*
>
> (Chinese elder, on life in an English speaking neighborhood)

What happens when children are the translators, the decoders, the messengers for their families? At Project LEIF, one tutor noted in his log that he wondered who was in charge when he found the home of his elder tutee plastered with heavy metal posters all over the house. A Lao teen sabotaged his mother's efforts to learn English, disrupting her English lessons and repeatedly telling her that she was too old to learn. One tutor reported that when she called her Vietnamese partner on the phone, the woman's son hovered on the line, as if English had become his domain to supervise and control. When this woman couldn't solve a homework problem, she let it go unaddressed rather than asking her children.

The issues of power and authority have an important impact on schooling. At Project LEIF, adults often reported to us their frustration at the degree to which they can (or cannot) help their children. At best, many wish they could help with their children's homework. At the least, some would like to understand the scope of the schoolwork, in order to know when their child has completed the assigned tasks. Many Asian parents report their fear of looking stupid to their children. Even when children are willing to be helpful, parents report their shame in having to depend on them.

Power shifts that occur through communication can be as uncomfortable for children as they are for adults. When Asian teens were asked to give advice to teachers at a local conference, one response was particularly poignant: "Please," commented a Vietnamese teen, "if I translate for you when you talk to my mother, don't look at me, look at her when you speak." This youth spoke of his embarrassment when his own mother was marginalized, and when he was treated like an authority in front of her.

These examples show that literacy events and speech events can be structured in ways to ascribe roles that are empowered or powerless for the interlocutors. The resulting shifts in power have consequences for children and adults alike. In order to invite adults to become part of their children's schooling, we need to become aware of the kinds of literacy and speech events that we unwittingly set up through our work. We also need to be aware of ways in which our interactions with families play into the evolving relationships of children and adults, especially as we operate on what slowly becomes the "linguistic turf" of the children.

Family Literacy: From School to Family Perspectives

The term *family literacy,* coined by Denny Taylor (1983) to describe the meanings and uses of literacy in families, is now more often used to describe programs that promote literacy development. In this section, I examine three sets of issues regarding family and intergenerational literacy. The first is that of experience: Whose experiences inform the work that we do and the mission that we set for ourselves? Second, I briefly mention some of the research that has recently gained attention to explore the issue of the questions we ask and how we search for answers. Third, I look directly at family and intergenerational program practices, with attention to whose agenda is being served through our work. For each of these themes, I propose moving beyond school perspectives and broadening our approach as we document experience, pose and pursue research questions, and create programs in which the purposes and concerns of families are central.

Experience: School voices, family voices

I visit them [the Cambodians] in their homes. I explain why it's important for them to come. I even call them the night before to remind them. "Yes," they say. "I'm coming." Then, next morning, I wait, no one comes. So I call them.

(Bilingual teacher)

This account sounds familiar because we know the experiences of hardworking, frustrated teachers. The shared experiences of teachers and administrators such as this one lie behind much intergenerational programming. Our instinct is to do what is necessary to fill the open houses and to get parents to help with homework. We want the children to do better in school, and we know that parents can make a difference.

Why is it that parents do not come? What is happening in these seemingly invisible families? What are the resources and constraints that shape the responses of adults? What are the strategies that parents use in supporting their children? With a family perspective on our programs, the experiences of school personnel are still important, but our work must also take into account the experiences of parents, grandparents, and children themselves. With an understanding of family resources and constraints, it becomes possible to know what is possible and what is appropriate when we ask adults to participate in our programs.

What educational resources have families brought with them? This varies widely from group to group. Koreans, for example, come from a country where 97% of the population is functionally literate (CDOE, 1992). In Korea, virtually all citizens have access to public education. As immigrants rather than refugees, Koreans had time to prepare, plan, and make their move with minimal stress and interruption to their own or their children's education. The move itself was often an attempt to improve educational opportunities.

In contrast, Cambodians with any educational experience were the first to be exterminated under the Pol Pot regime. Those who escaped from Cambodia either had little education or were able to pretend effectively that they had not. Centuries of literature were destroyed. During years in flight, many refugees began their educational experiences in refugee camps. Depending on the time spent in the camp and the setup of the camp's educational program, a variety of educational experiences were available to different refugee groups. Literacy and schooling are not always synonymous. Many Hmong refugees from Laos, despite a history of inexperience with formal schooling, have been quite successful at learning Hmong literacy through informal channels, such as one-on-one teaching by family members.

For adults who do not have histories of educational experience, despite their dreams for their children, reading English storybooks and helping their children with their homework are simply not options. In her research among Mexican parents, Delgado-Gaitan (1987) documents the hopes and frustrations of Mexican parents who desperately want something better for their children. She demonstrates the ways in which these adults provide supports within the limits of their resources in a system that does not tap into their potential for more substantial involvement. Just as Southeast Asians may have sold their most precious commodity, land, to send one child to school in Asia, so now many families find ingenious ways to support their children despite their own limited educational and literacy resources. One Hmong clan, the Lors, decided at a meeting in Nebraska to hold parties for Lor children all over the country, giving them a quarter for each "A" earned in school. These adults, not literate themselves, are grappling with creative ways to support their children's success in school.

In order to invite adults to participate in their children's schooling, it is helpful to have some information about relationships among teachers, parents, and children in the country of origin. For many Asian immigrants, such as the Lao, although high value is placed on education, it is considered the teachers' responsibility to provide the moral and spiritual education of children. Cambodians refer to teachers as the "second parent" who is entrusted with the child's care. The same parents who do not show up at open house come from a country where it is seen as inappropriate for parents to intervene in any way with the teacher's job (CDOE, 1988). Families such as these may be quite puzzled when they are invited to give input. The passive role of parents may be exacerbated by language barriers and lack of understanding of the American school system.

A second consideration for program planners and recruiters is the set of sociolinguistic rules governing behavior between children and adults. Among Hmong refugees, children learn by observing adults and by talking with peers. Conversations between children and adults are not the norm. One researcher comments that not only are Filipino children not to be heard, they are also to remain unseen. According to Jocano, "strict obedience and discipline are demanded and bred by the parent of the child" (CDOE, 1986, p. 34). Some of the interactions that occur in American educational programs may seem inappropriate to adults and children who are operating under unspoken rules that require children to signal respect by repressing their own ideas and desires in the presence of adults.

A third issue to consider is the need to be sensitive when offering to teach parenting skills. It is easy to forget that the groups from which immigrant learners come have been parenting effectively for centuries. It can certainly be argued that before the disruptions of displacement, many immigrant families had more experience than most Americans with maintaining strong extended families, raising secure children, and creating family support networks that nurture children and elders alike.

Whereas adults may have been very effective parents in their previous contexts, strategies that worked in one setting may no longer respond to the realities of new contexts. Parenting in the United States can be quite baffling for some newcomers, who may feel that parental authority is limited by law (e.g., regarding corporal punishment), yet schools and other societal systems are not up to the task of keeping kids in line. Back in the homeland, families often had the resources of the full community for dealing with the problems of their children, but there is no such support in a setting where the problems may be more serious and complicated. Adults may look on with horror as their children dabble with drugs or join city gangs in neighborhoods where few positive alternatives exist for youth. Cambodian adults often complain that their children threaten to call a child abuse hotline and have them taken to jail if they strike them. At a family literacy effort in Western Massachusetts, after a program session on child abuse, one Cambodian man joked that he preferred to have a session on parent abuse (Weinstein-Shr, 1992).

For adults to come to grips with raising their children in a new setting, it is not enough to teach them how to do things the way Americans do. Adults need a setting where they can gather information about their new environment and evaluate for themselves both traditional and new strategies for dealing with discipline, with school, or with other complex issues involved in raising children in a complicated world. This is made possible when the adults work with educators who believe they have as much to learn as they do to teach. The experiences of adults before resettlement and after, in the realities of our rural and urban neighborhoods, must become part of what we consider in providing family literacy support that makes sense.

Research: School questions, family questions

Research from a school perspective has as its driving concern the primary question: How can we help children do better in school? Educational research from several domains indicates the importance of parents in the school achievement of their children. Scholars of emergent literacy point to evidence that conceptual development happens during the earliest years in life (Teale, 1982; Teale & Sulzby, 1986) and emphasize parents as the "first teacher." Children's achievement in school has been demonstrated to be directly correlated with the mother's level of education (Sticht & McDonald, 1989). In addition, it is clear that parental behaviors, such as ways of "scaffolding" (i.e., constructing conversations), ways of talking about pictures in books, ways of telling bedtime stories, and other ways of interacting around print are important factors in predicting children's school success (Heath, 1982).

The impact of parents and home environment has also been a recent focus of scholars interested in language minority children. Attempts to understand school achievement have focused on early literacy and language at home (Cochran-Smith, 1984) and on other school-home differences (Cummins, 1981; Moll & Díaz, 1987). Results of these studies have been aimed at helping educators understand differences in order to sensitize teachers and to facilitate academic learning.

With the addition of a family perspective to a program's focus, other research questions also become important. Children's achievement in school becomes only one part of the picture. There are models of research that seek, as part of their goal, to illuminate the perspectives of adults who wish to acquire literacy. Gillespie (1993) gives a brief summary of qualitative research that explores perspectives of second-language learners in terms of their purposes for learning language and literacy, and how they view themselves in that process. Ethnographic work of Reder (1987) in four ethnic communities illustrates the possibilities for broadening concepts of literacy as we examine functions in diverse settings. Taylor and Dorsey-Gaines's (1988) work among African Americans illustrates the enormous resources families must have to get by in a bureaucratic world that relentlessly hurls obstacles in their path. A study by Rockhill (1990) among Latinas in Los Angeles raises provocative questions about the cost of literacy, as learning to read challenges existing relationships. Rockhill found that women's aspirations for literacy were often met with violence from their partners. These studies provide examples of how we can examine the role of literacies in the lives of adults and the consequences that literacy practices have for their lives and their relationships, both with their children and with other adults.

Specific studies of language use in families may hold the most promise for gaining useful insights for practical work. Researchers such as Fillmore (1991), for example, warn that where language loss was once a three-generational process, recent inquiry seems to indicate that in families where children attend English- language or bilingual preschools, the process has been accelerated to two generations, resulting in generations of parents and children who have difficulty talking with one another. Immersion in English at too early an age, she suggests, can be devastating to family relationships if support for native language development is lacking. If this analysis is correct, not only are immigrant children losing the chance to tap the resources of their grandparents, they are also losing a language of communication with parents. This gives some urgency to our mission; there is important work to be done. We know very little about the processes by which uprooted families manage their new lives and the crucial role of language and literacy in that process.

If research is to take into account the perspectives of families, it must address the themes that emerge from their lives. The questions below provide an example of areas we might explore.

1. Survival

• How do refugees and immigrants (or any families served by schools) solve or fail to solve problems that require literacy skills? (This requires that we seek to discover the resources they have, in addition to knowing what they lack.)

2. Communication

• What are the functions and uses of literacy (both native and second language) in the lives of people that are served?

• Who uses which language with whom and under what circumstances?

• What are the consequences of this particular set of communicative practices?

• What is the implication for home-school communications (including the parents' experiences of those communications)?

3. Power/authority

• What is the significance of language in the negotiation of new roles and relationships in a new setting?

• How has authority and power shifted in families?

• What is the role of language in intergenerational relationships?

• What are the ways in which schools influence the process in which these relationships are negotiated?

These are not questions for researchers alone, but also for teachers, program planners, and learners themselves to explore through family literacy work. The nature of that work is explored below.

Programs and practices: School agendas, family agendas

Schools play a critical role in the lives of families and in the future of the children who are growing up in America. Part of our mission, undoubtedly, as family literacy practitioners, is to demystify American schools for immigrants, to provide information about the ways schools work, and to communicate effectively to parents the expectations that teachers and administrators have of them. It is in everyone's interest that parents understand schools and have the best tools possible to support their children's success.[3] With a family perspective on education, it also becomes important to demystify immigrant families for schools, to provide information to school personnel about the most pressing issues of families and communities, and to communicate effectively to teachers and administrators the concerns and expectations of adults whose children are in their hands.

---

[3] For more information on programs with these goals, see the introduction to Section I of this volume and Weinstein-Shr (1990).

One promising model for encouraging adults to articulate their concerns, beliefs, and desires is the development of "parent circles," where adults meet to discuss their parenting concerns in their own language. These are patterned after study circles, which are "voluntary, informal, democratic, and highly participatory groups that assist members in understanding issues and in making choices" (Habana-Hefner, n.d., p. 1). When there is a safe place to think with others about difficult issues, adults often find strength through articulating their own perspectives and developing a collective voice. In this way, it becomes possible to speak (sometimes through culture brokers) to institutions such as schools, which may seem intimidating to parents as lone individuals. When schools, communities, and families are truly partners, the learning and adaptation goes both ways. As Quintero and Macías (1992) demonstrate, when parents and teachers are assisted in understanding the nature and value of one another's potential contributions, children are the first to benefit, while schools and communities are strengthened in the process.

A family perspective also requires that we examine the consequences of our work on the quality of life for children and adults in terms of the nature of their evolving relationships outside school. Twymon (1990), for example, found that when parent-child interaction centered around school-like tasks such as reenactment of reading lessons, the children initially did well in school. Over time, however, children began to experience tension, anger, hostility, resistance, and alienation in their home relationships (cited in Willett & Bloome, 1993).

Insights on the experience of children and adults in families can inform practice that aims at supporting the educational achievement of children without undermining the family as a crucial resource for adaptation. The Foxfire experiment demonstrated the possibilities for enabling children to strengthen their literacy skills while documenting and valuing the collective knowledge and experience of their families and communities (Wigginton, 1985). In this project, children from the hills of Appalachia collected recipes, folk tales, instructions for making banjos, and so forth by interviewing elders and creating documents that would preserve this information for their future children and their children's children. Innovative educators are beginning to rediscover the power of acknowledging what Moll (1992) calls community "funds of knowledge." Navajo parents who are unable to read in any language are often wonderful storytellers who can captivate their children with tales and who can listen to their children tell or read stories. Latino adults in the Pajaro Valley have become more interested in learning to read and in sharing literacy experiences with their children because of an emphasis on Spanish literature in addition to English (Ada, 1988).

When schools can capitalize on these funds of knowledge, literacy skills are developed and relationships are nurtured in synergy. As emphasis is placed on what can be done and what can be shared rather than on what is not done or what is not shared, children and adults can develop ways of being together in which they stretch, learn, and profit from one another. One experiment showed that children who read to their parents improved their reading skills as much as a control group who received equal hours of academic tutoring in reading (Tizard, Schofield, & Hewison, 1982). It is not hard to imagine that uprooted adults might find more pleasure in listening to their children read than in struggling to read aloud in a language they have not yet mastered.

Although steps have been taken to use insight into the family for improving school achievement, the next logical step is to use knowledge of schooling and learning processes to strengthen families and communities as resources for their members. With a family perspective, the consequences of educational practice will be measured not only by achievement test scores, but also by measures of the extent to which families and communities are sources of cooperative problem solving, provide mutual support for learning, and respect the resources of the generations. The accounts in this volume illustrate some of the attempts to move in this direction. With the challenges that our children will face for solving global problems, team work and cooperation between the generations are our best hope.

Learning from Uprooted Families: Blueprint for Inquiry

In this chapter I argue that our view from the classroom provides an extremely limited lens from which to reach out effectively to multilingual families and communities. I suggest that those who provide intergenerational programs in multilingual communities may wish to learn about certain aspects of the families and communities they serve:

1. The structure and characteristics of the community where participating families are members;

2. The language, literacy, and educational profiles of communities and community members; and

3. The most pressing concerns of adults in their role as parents, grandparents, or caretakers.

These issues may be explored together by family literacy staff members in a formal way through collaborative work with ethnic leaders and organizations or through the course of daily work both inside and outside the classrooms themselves. The following pages present a summary worksheet for educational providers who are interested in taking an inquiring stance toward these issues. The themes in the worksheet are suggested as beginning points; they may not be the most important ones for the communities that we wish to serve. In order to serve immigrant children and adults, we need to invite them to teach us about themselves:

• Their linguistic, cultural, and problem-solving resources;

• How they did things before they came to the United States and how they are managing now;

• The meanings and uses of language and literacy in their lives;

• The sense they are making of their current situation.

An inquiring stance may be humbling, because we can no longer pretend we know exactly what to do. But the rewards are many, not least of which is the escape from getting bureaucratic and bored. Most important, by inviting families to teach us about their perspectives, their language use, their communities, and their lives, we create a partnership that holds the most promise for joyfully linking the generations through our work.

Learning from Uprooted Families
Summary Worksheet

*1. Structure and characteristics of refugee
and immigrant communities*

A. Diversity

- In the communities we wish to serve, in what ways are members diverse?
- How are divisions expressed in the communities?
- What are the groups and subgroups?

B. Community leaders and other key players

- Who are members of the families we wish to serve? How do they themselves perceive family boundaries?
- What are kin patterns and social networks that influence how people manage?
- Who are the caretakers for children in the families we wish to serve?

*2. Language, literacy, and education:
Community and individual profiles*

A. History

- What were the educational experiences of target families in their homelands?
- What were the circumstances of flight and the nature of interruptions in schooling?
- What is the history of experience with native language literacy?

B. Language use in the community: Current practices

- What are attitudes toward native language literacy in the target community?
- What are the supports for native language development and use among children and adults?
- What are parents' language and literacy goals for themselves and for their children?
- How can our educational efforts support native language development?

C. Roles of teachers, parents, and children

- What is the traditional relationship of teachers and parents in the country of origin for the community we wish to serve?
- What are the norms for interaction between adults and children in this community?
- How do our program activities fit, or not fit, these norms?
- What are possible avenues for adjustment or negotiation?

3. Addressing the concerns of adults

A. Surviving trauma

- What were the circumstances of departure from the country of origin?
- What are some of the losses associated with this departure?
- What material and social resources are available for coping with change and loss?

B. Parenting in a dangerous world

- What are the conditions in which newcomers are raising their children?
- What are the key issues for newcomers and old timers alike in the schools and neighborhoods served?
- What are traditional means of disciplining children, and to what extent are they appropriate or possible in the United States?

C. Changing roles, changing relationships

- How are relationships changing among parents, grandparents, and children as a result of resettlement in a new country? Between men and women? Elders and youth?
- What is the role of language and literacy in these changes?
- How can our literacy work play a positive role in families where social conditions challenge even the healthiest of intergenerational relationships?

4. General queries for programming

- How much do we know about the families and communities we serve? How can we learn more both inside and outside our classrooms?
- What is the role of learners' native knowledge and personal experience in our programs and classrooms?
- What are possibilities through our programs for helping adults gather information about the school system, drugs, discipline, child abuse laws, or any other concerns they may have?
- What are their concerns specifically about their children's schooling?
- What opportunities do our programs provide for adults to discuss their concerns, compare the United States with their homelands, and get support from one another in grappling with complex problems?

References

Ada, A.F. (1988). The Pajaro Valley experience: Working with Spanish-speaking parents to develop children's reading and writing skills in the home through the use of children's literature. In T. Skutnabb-Kangas & J. Cummins (Eds.), *Minority education: From shame to struggle* (pp. 223-239). Philadelphia: Multilingual Matters.

California Department of Education. (1984). *Handbook for teaching Cantonese-speaking students*. Sacramento, CA: Author. (ERIC Document Reproduction Service No. ED 253 117)

California Department of Education. (1986). *Handbook for teaching Pilipino-speaking students*. Sacramento, CA: Author. (ERIC Document Reproduction Service No. ED 280 281)

California Department of Education. (1988). *Handbook for teaching Khmer-speaking students*. Sacramento, CA: Author. (ERIC Document Reproduction Service No. ED 325 581)

California Department of Education. (1992). *Handbook for teaching Korean-American students*. Sacramento, CA: Author. (ERIC Document Reproduction Service No. ED 342 248)

Cochran-Smith, M. (1984). *The making of a reader*. Norwood, NJ: Ablex.

Cummins, J. (1981). The role of primary language development in promoting educational success for language minority students. In J. Cummins (Ed.), *Schooling and language minority students: A theoretical framework* (pp. 3-50). Los Angeles: California State University.

Delgado-Gaitan, C. (1987). Mexican adult literacy: New directions for immigrants. In S.R. Goldman & H. Trueba (Eds.), *Becoming literate in English as a second language* (pp. 9-32). Norwood, NJ: Ablex.

Fillmore, L.W. (1991). When learning a second language means losing the first. *Early Research Quarterly, 6*, 323-346.

Fingeret, A. (1983). Social network: A new perspective on independence and illiterate adults. *Adult Education Quarterly, 33*, 133-146.

Gillespie, M. (1993). Revealing the multiple faces of literacy: Profiles of adult learners. *TESOL Quarterly, 27,* 529-532.

Habana-Hefner, S. (n.d.). *Addressing parenting and educational issues of Cambodian women in Lowell.* Unpublished manuscript.

Heath, S.B. (1982). What no bedtime story means: Narrative skills at home and at school. *Language in Society 2*(2), 49-76.

McKay, S., & Weinstein-Shr, G. (1993). English literacy in the United States: National policies, personal consequences. *TESOL Quarterly, 27,* 399-420.

Moll, L. (1992). Bilingual classroom studies and community analyses: Some recent trends. *Educational Researcher, 20,* 20-24.

Moll, L., & Díaz, R. (1987). Teaching writing as communication: The use of ethnographic findings in classroom practice. In D. Bloome (Ed.), *Literacy and schooling* (pp. 195-222). Norwood, NJ: Ablex.

Quintero, E., & Macías, A. (1992). Families learning together: Sociocultural issues in literacy. *Journal of Educational Issues for Language Minority Students, 10,* 41-56.

Reder, S. (1987). Comparative aspects of functional literacy development: Three ethnic American communities. In D. Wagner (Ed.), *The future of literacy in a changing world* (pp. 250-270). New York: Pergamon.

Rockhill, K. (1990). Literacy as threat/desire: Longing to be somebody. *TESL Talk, 20*(1), 89-109.

Sticht, T.G., & McDonald, B.A. (1989). *Making the nation smarter: The intergenerational transfer of cognitive ability.* San Diego: Institute for the Study of Adult Literacy.

Taylor, D. (1983). *Family literacy: Young children learning to read and write.* Exeter, NH: Heinemann.

Taylor, D., & Dorsey-Gaines, C. (1988). *Growing up literate: Learning from inner-city families.* Portsmouth, NH. Heinemann.

Teale, W.H. (1982). Reading to young children: Its significance for literacy development. In H. Goelman, A. Oberg, & F. Smith (Eds.), *Awakening to literacy* (pp. 110-121). Portsmouth, NH: Heinemann.

Teale, W., & Sulzby, E. (Eds.). (1986). *Emergent literacy: Writing and reading.* Norwood, NJ: Ablex.

Tizard, J., Schofield, W., & Hewison, J. (1982). Symposium: Reading collaboration between teachers and parents in assisting children's reading. *British Journal of Educational Psychology, 52*, 1-15.

Twymon, S. (1990). *Early reading and writing instruction in the homes and schools of three five-year old children from black working class families.* Unpublished doctoral dissertation, University of Michigan, Ann Arbor.

Weinstein-Shr, G. (1989, October). Breaking the linguistic and social isolation of refugee elders. *TESOL News, 9,* 17.

Weinstein-Shr, G. (1990). From problem-solving to celebration: Creating and discovering meanings through literacy. *TESL Talk, 20*(1), 68-88.

Weinstein-Shr, G. (1992). *Language use in refugee families: Cambodian parents in focus.* (Final report to the Spencer Foundation). Amherst, MA: University of Massachusetts.

Weinstein-Shr, G. (1993). Literacy and social process: A community in transition. In B. Street (Ed.), *Cross-cultural approaches to literacy* (pp. 272-293). Cambridge, England: Cambridge University Press.

Weinstein-Shr, G., & Lewis, N. (1991). Language, literacy and the older refugee in America: Research agenda for the nineties. *College ESL, 1*(1), 53-65.

Wigginton, E. (1985). *Sometimes a shining moment: The Foxfire experience.* Garden City, NY: Anchor/Doubleday.

Willett, J., & Bloome, D. (1993). Literacy, language, school and community: A community-centered view. In A. Carrasquilo & C. Hedley (Eds.), *Whole language and the bilingual learner* (pp. 35-57). Norwood, NJ: Ablex.

CHAPTER 10

Evidence of Success: Learner Assessment and Program Evaluation in Innovative Programs

Heide Spruck Wrigley

> *Not everything that's measured counts, and*
> *not everything that counts can be measured.*

The projects and programs profiled in this volume show the depth and richness of family literacy programs. Yet it is this very complexity that makes it difficult to assess learner progress and evaluate program success by conventional means. Many, if not most of the changes that occur as learners awaken to literacy cannot be captured by tests, nor can the effects that programs have on their communities be demonstrated through a standard pre/post evaluation design. To remedy this situation, innovative programs are looking for alternative ways to show that they are making a difference.

Several chapters in this book illustrate this point. Dan Doorn, for example, tells us about Daniel, the young boy who wanted to tell about his trip to Mexico. Daniel, who is part of a journal writing project, chose to dictate his story to his cousin, rather than struggle through the mechanics of putting his story on paper. The way Doorn tells the story, it is easy to see that Daniel became a writer that summer, in the sense that he found a story worth telling, composed it, and shared it with an audience. Yet if Daniel were to take a conventional writing test, his success would not be immediately apparent. As is the case with many beginning writers, Daniel may even score worse on a posttest than he did on a pretest, and a less insightful teacher might have branded his dictating his story as cheating. Yet through portfolios, observations, and descriptions of Daniel's writing stages, it is possible to get a sense of how learners such as Daniel grow as writers.

Nora Lewis and Cecilia Varbero (Project LEIF) and Jessica Dilworth (Sunnyside UP) tell a slightly different story as they discuss challenges in program implementation. Yet they, too, illustrate the mismatch between program reality and standard evaluation designs. Both accounts show that there were hits and misses in communication and understanding between literacy partners that made program implementation difficult. A conventional evaluation based on a comparison between implementation plans and program outcomes might negatively reflect on the amount of time it took for these projects to build a common understanding of goals and purposes. However, it is their initial failures to communicate that have contributed to the success of these programs. By chronicling their struggles, these projects provide the kind of documentation that shows how difficult it is to take literacy beyond the classroom and into the community. By sharing their experience through project accounts, they also help other programs to set more realistic expectations about community collaborations.

These examples give us a glimpse of the shortcomings of conventional assessments. What teachers have known for some time is becoming more obvious as we see more researchers involved in ethnographies and case studies. Standardized tests and evaluations that look at narrow indicators of success present only a partial (and in many cases untrue) picture of program success. What's more, they threaten to trivialize literacy work, fail to capture the richness of learning so evident to staff and learners, and miss many of the changes that occur in participants' lives. Innovative programs now face the challenge of developing assessment models that truly reflect the nature of their programs and bear witness to the successes they experience and the challenges they face.

Challenges to Assessment and Evaluation

Even under the best of circumstances, learner assessment and program evaluation can be daunting tasks for family literacy programs. In many cases, the challenges of everyday operations and day-to-day teaching take up most of the time and energy that staff have available. In addition, funds for program evaluation often go to outside evaluators, while staff time needed for the evaluation is not compensated. As a result, teachers may resent the demands on their time that systematic assessment and evaluation require. Yet, many of these teachers have become natural evaluators, observing their students, listening to their concerns, and responding to the progress they see on a daily basis. They know about risk and frustration; they have come to understand their students' "ways of knowing"; and they are ready to celebrate literacy magic when it happens (see Quintero, this volume.)

In observing literacy classes across the country and talking to teachers and learners about their successes, I have been struck by the richness of learning and the breadth of literacy practices that are evident in many innovative programs. However, as an evaluator and regular visitor to a number of programs, I have one wish. I wish teachers could be enticed to document progress in a more systematic fashion, so that the magic that happens can be studied and evaluated. I wish there were an easy way to share with others in the literacy field the vast amount of knowledge that exists in the hearts and minds of teachers. In a field that suffers from lack of proof of program effectiveness, such knowledge, made public, could lead to greater respect for literacy educators and possibly more funds for teacher-led research. In the meantime, I understand the frustration of the Massachusetts funder who, when told by a teacher that she did no formal assessment because she could "feel" that her students were making progress, told her, "You can't send that to Springfield" (Balliro, 1989).

Administrators face similar challenges in showing program-wide evidence of success. The very nature of innovative programs makes it difficult to carry out an evaluation that measures effectiveness by conventional means, that is, by comparing program objectives and program outcomes. As educators working in nontraditional programs have known for some time, objectives that were set initially (and helped to get the program funded) change over time as the realities of program implementation take over. As programs get underway, some goals may expand, while others may need to be scaled back, and still others may need to be added. In many innovative programs, the standard evaluation question, "To what extent has the program met its objectives?", is difficult if not impossible to answer. Evaluations are particularly challenging in participatory programs where both curriculum and learner objectives emerge as the program progresses (see Auerbach, 1992; McGrail, this volume).

Developing an Assessment and Evaluation Framework

As practitioners know, assessing learner progress and documenting program success in innovative programs can be both exhilarating and wearying—exhilarating because it leads to new insights about language, literacy, and learning, and wearying because it takes so much time to get it right. In talking to teachers who believe in active learning and programs that support teaching, I see potential for developing evaluation designs that show what is working and what needs mending and, at the same time, providing our constituencies (families, schools, legislatures, funders) with enough information to reassure them that project monies have been well spent.

During the last few years, I have worked with teachers and coordinators in ESL literacy programs to help them develop an evaluation framework that can guide their individual assessment efforts and help them make decisions about where to focus their energies. The framework is taking shape as we go along, and, as with literacy, it develops in fits and spurts—two steps forward, one step back. We do not expect this framework ever to be finished nor do we want it to be, but as more and more literacy educators explore issues of assessment (Auerbach, 1992; Balliro, 1989; Fingeret, 1993; Gelardi, 1994; Holt, 1994; Lytle & Wolfe, 1989; McGrail, 1992; Ramírez, 1994), the ideas are taking shape. I believe that an assessment framework, adapted to local contexts, can serve as a decision-making tool that allows programs to focus on their strengths, helps them to address their weaknesses, and tells those outside of the program that family literacy education is making a difference.

I present the emergent framework here as a series of questions designed to help programs decide how they want to shape their evaluation efforts. I focus on those parts of the framework that I believe will help programs get started:

1. Articulation of a literacy perspective;

2. Description of goals and expectations;

3. Linkages among goals, curriculum, and assessment; and

4. Definitions of success and the development of standards.

Examples of actual assessments appear throughout the discussion. (For fuller treatment of the framework, see Wrigley, 1991, 1992, 1994.)

Perspective: What Do We Mean by Family Literacy?

Family literacy programs must come to a common understanding of what family literacy is (or should be) about. Deciding what the project means by literacy in general and by family literacy in particular will help us decide which assessments make sense. Many family literacy programs, for example, have shifted from seeing literacy as a set of decoding and encoding skills toward a view of literacy as a set of practices that are shaped by the social context in which they occur (Weinstein-Shr, 1992). As a result, more and more programs have begun to examine the social contexts in which learners use or want to use literacy. They now see language and literacy development as a holistic process of "meaning making," rather than as the acquisition of a set of basic skills that can be measured in discrete units. They emphasize the multifaceted nature of literacy, seeking to involve learners in a broad range of literacy experiences and practices, both familiar and new (Wrigley & Guth, 1992).

In addition to taking a much broader perspective on literacy, a number of programs now teach literacy in two languages: in English and in the mother tongue of the learners. In doing so, they also seek to examine the contexts in which one or both of the languages are used and to explore the practices that bilingual adults use to negotiate their environments. These changing perspectives of what we mean by language, literacy, and learning are perhaps the most significant reason that assessment schemes that rely on the standardized tests presently in existence are inadequate measures of success for most family literacy programs (Auerbach, 1992; Lytle & Wolfe, 1989; Wrigley, 1994). To truly capture the nature of a program, evaluations need to reflect the program's vision.

Goals and Expectations: Why Are We Doing This?

As a rule, family literacy programs seek to achieve both short-term and long-terms goals. For most programs, the overriding goal is literacy development for adults, children, and their families. Some programs, such as the federally funded Family English Literacy Programs (FELPs), include the increased school achievement of language minority children as part of their long-term goals. In programs that serve families who speak a language other than English (immigrants, refugees, migrants from Puerto Rico, Native Americans), an additional goal is to foster acquisition of English as a second language (ESL) and bridge the gap between the culture of the home and the culture of school. To do so, some programs, like the National Council of La Raza FELP project in Los Angeles and Project FIEL in El Paso, also taught literacy in the primary language of the participants and used a bilingual and cross-cultural approach to literacy development. None of these goals is easily captured by conventional assessments.

In many cases, language and literacy development is only one part of the overall mission of the project. To fully meet the needs of the communities they serve, many programs include social goals along with linguistic goals. Project LEIF in Philadelphia, for example, is a tutor-based project that seeks to promote literacy and foster understanding among diverse ethnic groups through the creation of cross-generational and cross-cultural relationships. Goals also include helping the elderly access existing health and social services and increasing the language proficiency of school-age children so they can function more effectively in school. In their evaluation, LEIF uses both quantitative measures (e.g., total number of tutor hours provided, number of learners served, and number of participants in special events) and qualitative measures (e.g., collecting and analyzing tutor comments written after each session, analyzing coordinator logs, and conducting periodic interviews with learners). Case studies of individual families and community ethnographies that span several years can provide an even richer picture of the changes that take place in individual learners and the community as a result of literacy involvement.

Project FIEL, funded from August 1988 to May 1991, had broad educational goals as well, including development of biliteracy curricula and strategies, and responsiveness to the social and cultural contexts of immigrant families. Specifically, the project sought to do the following:

1. Enhance the literacy and biliteracy development of children through a series of participatory intergenerational activities;

2. Provide information regarding the literacy development process in children to the parents in a setting that allows parents to use this information;

3. Enhance parents' self-confidence in helping their children; and

4. Empower parents to connect literacy activities to their own social/cultural situations.

Project FIEL used portfolios, case studies, and classroom observations to chart programs and provide evidence of success.

Program Design and Curriculum: What Will Get Us There?

As this volume shows, the greatest strengths of innovative family literacy programs may be their comprehensive program design and their rich curriculum. In linking families, schools, and communities, many seek to address the personal, social, linguistic, and cognitive aspects of literacy, whereas others include the political and economic dimensions of literacy as well. No matter which dimensions are emphasized, these programs share a common goal: to deliver rich opportunities for learners to become familiar with "many literacies" (Gillespie, 1990). To that end, they provide encounters with literacy that give families chances to read and write, discuss and share, challenge and be challenged, and make mistakes and learn from them. In many of these programs, families also learn to argue and justify, to develop hypotheses and test them, to access resources, and to act as a resource to others.

How is this accomplished? Many programs provide this opportunity through project work such as developing family histories, producing *foto-novelas*, writing autobiographies, producing yearbooks, or publishing resource guides to services in the community. Others set up health fairs, potlucks, or swap meets or organize food or sewing co-ops. Still others take an advocacy stand, working with parents to set up bilingual PTAs or helping them to fight for changes in their schools or their communities. Innovative programs also provide learners with opportunities in the classroom to explore ideas and experiences through literacy. In these classrooms, families gain confidence in different ways of reading (reading for fun, reading to learn, reading to do) and learn to express their ideas in different forms, through storytelling or poems, art or music, family trees and photos of special events, histories and biographies, timelines, and story webs (see also Auerbach, 1992; Bell & Burnaby, 1984; Nash, Cason, Rhum, McGrail, & Gómez-Sanford, 1992; Wrigley & Guth, 1992). Quite clearly, if we want to document the effectiveness of new designs and the success of innovative approaches, we need to develop assessments that protect the integrity of our teaching and capture the richness of our curricula.

Standards: What Counts as Success?

I believe that this question, which goes to the crux of alternative assessment, presents the greatest challenge to literacy programs. Our definitions of success need to be refined and, in many cases, defined, if we wish to provide counterarguments to the (not unfounded) contention that literacy programs lack both rigor and proof of effectiveness (Alamprese, 1988; Diekhoff, 1988).

Success can be defined either in qualitative terms, through descriptions of learner accomplishments, or in quantitative terms by measuring, for example, levels of participation in various events or degrees of learner satisfaction with program activities. For example, a program might deem a workshop successful if 60% of enrollees participated, and 75% of participants found the information presented useful or interesting. In new programs, these numbers may need to be adjusted several times, because some learners are much less likely to attend than others, and some groups tend to be much more critical than their more sanguine counterparts. If the numbers a new project has set for itself turn out to be widely off the mark, it is important to examine the circumstances so that it becomes evident where adjustments are necessary. Generally, we can come to one of two conclusions: Either we had set our sights too high and need to become more realistic, or the activities we offered did not meet the needs of the learners and need be changed. Surveys and interviews with participants, supplemented by coordinator comments, can provide rich data that tell us why some project activities have been widely successful while others have bombed. We need to find out what works, for whom, under what circumstances.

A mixture of quantitative and qualitative assessments can also show what kind of success we are achieving by involving learners in innovative literacy activities. For example, literacy profiles that include reading logs, reader response sheets, learner-generated writings, and developmental checklists along with peer assessments and teacher comments can provide rich data on both the processes and the products of writing.

As research with portfolio-based assessments has shown (Valencia, 1990), these measures are most successful when accompanied by evaluation rubrics that clearly outline the assessment criteria to be used. These criteria can be accompanied by writing samples that show what *beginning, intermediate*, or *proficient* writers may create as they become involved in literacy. When such evaluation rubrics are used to compare initial portfolios (collected during the first two weeks of a course) with progress portfolios (created toward the end of a cycle), we can clearly see growth in significant areas of literacy development.

For example, stories that may appear flat at first often turn into powerful accounts of life experiences as learners become more confident and find their own voice as writers. Similarly, entries in dialogue journals, often quite skimpy during the first few weeks of class, may brim with rich details during the end of the course, thus providing evidence of progress in literacy as well as testifying to the fact that readers and writers have come to trust each other.

By designating certain characteristics of good writing (such as authenticity and voice, richness of expression, clarity of thought) as goals to be achieved, program staff can help learners understand that literacy development at any level involves standards worth aspiring to. By inviting participants in family literacy programs to share experiences that have moved them or to discuss issues that are close to their hearts, we as teachers can provide new writers with the opportunity to internalize and meet these standards.

Evaluation Measures: How Do We Know We Are Successful?

Definition and determination of success are also made difficult by the fact that innovative programs are moving from a "rationalistic paradigm," in which program objectives are compared to program outcomes toward a "naturalistic paradigm" that relies on ethnographic descriptions of what happens as a program unfolds. Although naturalistic evaluations tend to be open-ended, leaving room for unintended outcomes, they nevertheless require that those who evaluate have a good idea of what they are looking for. To be successful, naturalistic evaluations must be valid; that is, the evaluator must be capable of making sound judgments that assure that she shares with program participants and funders an understanding of what counts as success. Quite often we cannot predict where we will encounter success, but we are quite unlikely to find it if we do not have a good sense of what it might look like. For example, a family literacy teacher who defines success as "parents reading to their children" is likely to miss the literacy development that occurs when children read to their parents.

In carrying out naturalistic evaluations, we also need to be cognizant of the question, "Who cares and what do they care about?", so that the concerns of all participants—teachers, learners, families, communities, and outside stakeholders—are taken into account. One promising attempt to answer this question has been to involve teachers, learners, and others as co-investigators in the assessment and evaluation process. For example, many programs involve families in a goal-setting process that allows them to articulate their expectations and define their own notions of success. Many times, community members are invited to visit the program and discuss what they see as benchmarks—achievements that make them sit up, take notice, and say, "Yeah, that's it. You people have really made a difference." Again, initial expectations of success may need to be revised as learners surprise us with their insights and accomplishments. For example, one of the most significant outcomes of literacy programs everywhere has been the increase in self-confidence that learners have experienced. The goal of strengthening learners' belief in their own ability to learn, to effect change, and to succeed in their efforts has become one of the major aims of innovative programs. As a result, learner assessments are now being developed to document and measure increases in self-confidence.

Defining success, setting standards, and developing benchmarks can be extremely difficult for first-year programs where program directors are not quite sure what results they might expect. Yet I believe that it is worth our efforts to sit down together and imagine the differences our programs can make. Our expectations can always be adjusted later. Asking ourselves questions such as, "What would make us proud of our program?" and "How do we get there?", makes us set high standards and helps us to create the kinds of educational opportunities that will make a difference in the lives of learners and in their communities. I very much believe that if we refuse to be accountable to any standard, even our own, others will set those standards for us, much to the detriment of nontraditional learners, creative teachers, and innovative programs.

References

Alamprese, J.A. (1988). *Adult literacy research and development: An agenda for action.* Washington, DC: Southport Institute for Policy Analysis. (ERIC Document Reproduction Service No. ED 302 676)

Auerbach, E.R. (1992). *Making meaning, making change: Participatory curriculum development for adult ESL literacy.* Washington, DC and McHenry, IL: Center for Applied Linguistics and Delta Systems.

Balliro, L. (1989, March). *Reassessing assessment in adult ESL/ literacy.* Paper presented at the international convention of Teachers of English to Speakers of Other Languages, San Antonio, TX. (ERIC Document Reproduction Service No. ED 339 253)

Bell, J., & Burnaby, B. (1984). *A handbook for ESL literacy.* Toronto: OISE Press.

Diekhoff, G.M. (1988). An appraisal of adult literacy programs: Reading between the lines. *Journal of Reading, 31,* 624-630.

Fingeret, H.A. (1993). *It belongs to me: A guide to portfolio assessment in adult education programs.* Durham, NC: Literacy South. (ERIC Document Reproduction Service No. ED 359 352)

Gelardi, S. (1994). Collecting, analyzing, and reporting alternative assessment results. In D.D. Holt (Ed.), *Assessing success in family literacy projects: Alternative approaches to assessment and evaluation.* Washington, DC and McHenry, IL: Center for Applied Linguistics and Delta Systems.

Gillespie, M. (1990). *Many literacies: Modules for training adult beginning readers and tutors.* Amherst, MA: University of Massachusetts, Center for International Education.

Holt, D.D. (1994). Introduction to alternative approaches to assessment and evaluation. In D.D. Holt (Ed.), *Assessing success in family literacy projects: Alternative approaches to assessment and evaluation.* Washington, DC and McHenry, IL: Center for Applied Linguistics and Delta Systems.

Lytle, S.L., & Wolfe, M. (1989). *Adult literacy education: Program evaluation and learner assessment.* Columbus, OH: ERIC Clearinghouse on Adult, Career, and Vocational Education. (ERIC Document Reproduction Service No. ED 315 665)

McGrail, L. (Ed.). (1992). *Adventures in Assessment.* Volume Two: Ongoing Assessment.

Nash, A., Cason, A., Rhum, M., McGrail, L., & Gómez-Sanford, R. (1992). *Talking shop: A curriculum sourcebook for participatory adult ESL.* Washington, DC and McHenry, IL: Center for Applied Linguistics and Delta Systems.

Ramírez, P. (1994). Integrating program planning, implementation, and evaluation. In D.D. Holt (Ed.), *Assessing success in family literacy projects: Alternative approaches to assessment and evaluation.* Washington, DC and McHenry, IL: Center for Applied Linguistics and Delta Systems.

Valencia, S. (1990). A portfolio approach to classroom reading: The whys, whats, and hows. *The Reading Teacher, 43,* 338-340.

Weinstein-Shr, G. (1992). *Family and intergenerational literacy in multilingual families. ERIC Q&A.* Washington, DC: Center for Applied Linguistics, National Clearinghouse on Literacy Education. (ERIC Document Reproduction Service No. ED 321 624)

Wrigley, H.S. (1991). *Alternative approaches to documenting progress in language learning and literacy development.* Paper submitted to the Workshop on Alternative Approaches to Evaluating English Family Literacy Programs. (ERIC Document Reproduction Service No. ED 333 7649)

Wrigley, H.S. (1992). *Learner assessment in adult ESL literacy. ERIC Q&A* Washington, DC: Center for Applied Linguistics, National Clearinghouse on Literacy Education. (ERIC Document Reproduction Service No. ED 353 863)

Wrigley, H.S. (1994). Assessing ongoing progress: Are we progressing? In D.D. Holt (Ed.), *Assessing success in family literacy projects: Alternative approaches to assessment and evaluation.* Washington, DC and McHenry, IL: Center for Applied Linguistics and Delta Systems.

Wrigley, H.S., & Guth, G.J.A. (1992). *Bringing literacy to life: Issues and options in adult ESL literacy.* San Mateo, CA: Aguirre International. (ERIC Document Reproduction Service No. ED 348 896)

CHAPTER 11
Magic and Risk: Lessons for the Future

Elizabeth Quintero

Magic and risk—these are unusual terms for a discussion of literacy. Yet, the family literacy and intergenerational collaborations described in this volume illuminate both magic and risk. I see important lessons in the projects described here for the future of all learning contexts, especially those appropriate for immigrant, multilingual, and multicultural learners. It is my contention, through following the literature on family literacy and following the stories of families—children and parents, toddlers and elders, teenagers and younger siblings, familiar friends and new friends—that some intergenerational programs have had the patent on magic over the past decade. Through these intergenerational programs, their struggles and their risks, we learn about educational programming and teaching practice.

These intergenerational programs have had the advantage of what I consider to be a natural form of magic. It is what sociologists and anthropologists call a positive social context, and what child developmentalists call unequivocable love between parent and child. In other words, magic happens because of what families across cultures do best—care for, attend to, and love each other, regardless of conditions. Weinstein-Shr (1994) portrays the magic in a loving social context when she imagines herself in Laos, not speaking the language or understanding the customs, but at the same time desperately trying to do what is best for her young daughter.

The magic made in intergenerational programs can be seen through comments by parents about themselves and their children. For example, a Mexican woman sums up her feelings at the close of a series of family literacy classes with her daughter: "I feel content, I can help with something worthwhile" (translated from Spanish, Project FIEL, El Paso, Texas). Another writes proudly, "I notice now that Grissel communicates more and she likes to write for herself.

Before Grissel wanted me to write everything because she would say she didn't know how to write" (translated from Spanish, Project FIEL, El Paso, Texas).

Furthermore, we have seen magic in many intergenerational programs because the people collaborating on family literacy projects have had to take risks and have grown in the process. For some of the parent participants, it is a risk to enter a school building in a foreign country where the expectations are unknown. Almost all parents risk disruptions in already busy and difficult family routines. In addition, for all parents, regardless of their background, the risk of addressing creativity, child development, and learning needs is a struggle. To decide when to help, how specifically to help with a learning task, and when to encourage independence in their children is a challenge. Yet, by working alongside one's child, the task becomes clearer. As one parent from Project FIEL says,

> *Today I'm learning about my children's creativity and understanding and helping them in whatever I can because I like to share the hour with my children...Here I feel comfortable and confident.*

(Translated from Spanish, Project FIEL, El Paso, Texas)

Children take risks too. In the excitement of working with parents and elders, some children have taken the risk of using innovative literacy practices. Some family literacy projects put aside the textbooks and use elders' storytelling as authentic history lessons. Other projects encourage children to discuss and value their cultural traditions and family routines. Some family literacy projects leave behind strict adherence to English grammar and writing rules and encourage the use of code-switching in both oral and written communication. In the example below, Diana, a kindergarten student in El Paso, Texas, chatted in writing about the valentine activity done in her family literacy class where codeswitching was encouraged.

Voy a mordir a Grandma with the love bug *porque le quiero.*

(I'm going to bite Grandma with the love bug because I love her.)

She spoke from the heart, but she also risked forgetting to use only English the next morning in her regular class setting, where she may be admonished for mixing Spanish and English.

Finally, we see risk on the part of teachers. Teachers in intergenerational programs have had to risk working with unfamiliar age groups and trying out newly developed lessons that have never been field tested. One teacher voiced in her journal the risks and rewards of teaching in a nontraditional setting with intergenerational groups:

> *I have witnessed growth within myself. This growth has been affected by the children. Because of them, I've pushed myself to provide interesting activities that are appropriate. My confidence increases with each opportunity. The family literacy project has provided me with unforgettable experiences. Working with parents has also added to my growth. I know with every experience comes change, and luckily mine have been positive. With change though, I always keep in mind to respect my students. For it is through respect that I will gain as well. Moreover, I accept and acknowledge them, because without them, growth would not result.*

Thus, it seems urgent that while continuing our intergenerational efforts in collaboration with the families we work with, we must advocate for change in other learning contexts as well. Those in other learning contexts have much to learn from our intergenerational family contexts, just as family literacy providers have learned to learn from observing, interacting with, and serving the diverse participants of our programs.

This discussion focuses on aspects of magic and risk in family literacy programs that I hope to see influencing other learning contexts for immigrant learners and their families as well:

• Magic in the form of respect for the knowledge and information that families bring with them to our programs. These alternative ways of knowing seem to mystify so many educators but are a part of each family's daily life. Magic is made when educators are informed by families' knowledge.

• Risk-taking in the form of collaboration that often "goes against the grain" (Cochran-Smith, 1991) of traditional practice. Risk-taking must be nurtured as we participate in the multidirectional transfer of knowledge. Children, parents, teachers, tutors, volunteers, care givers, and policymakers are all educators and all learners when risk-taking and collaboration are encouraged.

Magic: Alternative Ways of Knowing

Alternative ways of knowing—alternatives to traditional Euro-American mainstream cultural norms—are persevering in some contexts through the practice of passing on family cultural traditions to children. Although anthropologists have sought to understand alternative ways of knowing for decades, educators have more recently given attention to this:

> Knowledge can come from many sources, and alternative ways of knowing can only add to our vision of issues...and [our] understanding of curriculum and pedagogy. It is useful to hear different voices tell their stories about how they experience education or schooling. (Bloch, 1991, p.106)

A whole language educator and bilingual scholar maintains that learning is best achieved through direct engagement and experience. Learners' purposes and intentions are what drives learning (Edelsky, 1990). When past and present experience and engagement in that experience occur in a family context, the learning is multidirectional—for adults, for children, and for teachers.

Parents have demonstrated the richness of their alternative knowledge in various intergenerational programs. A program designed for American Indian parents in Minnesota compares parenting styles and family values of Indian parents with those of mainstream Anglo culture. The knowledge of both groups is attended to and included. For example, the lengthy list (Richardson, in Stuecher, 1991) of differences developed by the adult learners includes the following:

Native American Indians	*Anglo Americans*
1. Happiness—this is paramount! Be able to laugh at misery; life is to be enjoyed.	1. Success—generally involving status, security, wealth, and proficiency.

2. Sharing—everything belongs to others, just as Mother Earth belongs to all people.

2. Ownership—prefer to own an outhouse rather than share a mansion.

3. Tribe and extended family first, before self.

3. "Think of Number One!" syndrome.

(pp. 8-9)

In an adult literacy class for Southeast Asian learners, during a lesson regarding family values and childrearing practices, Asian students juxtaposed their views and cultural values with those of Americans:

Asians	*Anglo-Americans*
Asians live in time.	Americans live in space.
Asians like to contemplate.	Americans like to act.
Asians live in peace with nature.	Americans try to impose their will on nature.
Religion is Asians' first love.	Technology is Americans' passion.
Asians believe in freedom of silence.	Americans believe in freedom of speech.
Asians are taught to want less.	Americans are urged every day to want more.

(ESL class, Adult Learning Center, Duluth, Minnesota)

This comparison of ways of knowing the world opens dialogue and informs newcomers about United States culture, yet does not force immigrants to forget or negate the importance of their own culture. The activity also provides information for American teachers about the world of the learners and how they see the host culture.

These alternative ways of knowing are being recognized by some policymakers. Oakes and Lipton (1990), California researchers whose work influences educational policy nationwide, explicitly state,

We believe that parents, policymakers, and schools need to look at how children learn naturally. This view will lead to lessons built on knowledge that is important, challenging, complex, related to real life, and rich in meaning. Furthermore, curricula grounded in complex knowledge stand the best chance of stretching the intellectual sensemaking of all children. (p. 95)

Specifically discussing curriculum, Oakes and Lipton (1990, pp. 94-106) maintain that a good lesson presents a problem, provides a context, uses knowledge from life as well as from books, is one where everybody helps, requires more active learning than passive learning, has children working together rather than alone, and should appeal to any curious learner of whatever age and skill.

Wouldn't lessons be easy to design if educators listened to the knowledge that adults and children grapple with in their lives? For example, in one family literacy class, children wrote about what is important in their lives:

Child O: Angel es m fnd. (Angel is my friend.)

Child A: I love my grandma.

Child V: I like truck to go camping.

Child M: *Me enojo cuando mi mamá me castiga.* (I am angry when my mother punishes me.)

Child M: *Me siento triste cuando mi mamá no me deja ir con mi amiga.* (I feel sad when my mother doesn't let me go with my friend.)

Child V: I get scar of monsters. (I get scared of monsters.)

These children love, laugh, get angry, and get scared. As Oakes and Lipton (1990) advise, personal meanings provide a rich point of departure for virtually any subject of study.

We have all had moments when our learners' ways of knowing have slipped by us, unnoticed. For example, Kingston (1989) tells a personal story about cultural knowledge, passed on through families, that was not attended to by an elementary teacher:

When my second grade class did a play, the whole class went to the auditorium except the Chinese girls. The teacher, lovely and Hawaiian, should have understood about us, but instead left us behind in the classroom. Our voices were too soft or nonexistent, and our parents never signed the permission slips, anyway. They never signed anything unnecessary....

I remember telling the Hawaiian teacher, "We Chinese can't sing 'land where our fathers died.' " She argued with me about politics, while I meant because of curses. (p.194)

The curses Kingston spoke of were unknown to the teacher. Therefore her reaction to her students' reluctance was innapropriate.

Robert Coles (1990) discusses how Hopi children's ways of knowing directly conflicted with both the knowledge and social context of the children's teachers.

Here, for example, is what I eventually heard from a ten-year-old Hopi girl I'd known for almost two years: "The sky watches us and listens to us. It talks to us, and it hopes we are ready to talk back. The sky is where the God of the Anglos lives, a teacher told us. She asked where our God lives. I said, 'I don't know.' I was telling the truth! Our God is the sky, and lives wherever the sky is. Our God is the sun and the moon, too; and our God is our people, if we remember to stay here. This is where we're supposed to be, and if we leave, we lose God." (p. 26)

Coles asked if she had explained the above to the teacher.

"No."

"Why?"

"Because, she thinks God is a person. If I'd told her, she'd give us that smile."

"What smile?"

"The smile that says to us, 'You kids are cute, but you're dumb; you're different, and you're all wrong!' " (p. 26)

These are examples of alternative ways of knowing that are not currently accepted in most school curricula. This is a loss to the children who bring this knowledge with them to schools as well as to the children whose understandings match those of their teachers. This is a loss to parents who want to pass on cultural traditions and ways of knowing but find themselves fighting not only the school information, but their children's beliefs about the value of their own ways of knowing. Furthermore, this is a loss to teachers, who could be opening new worlds of exploration to children and themselves while providing a bridge between the culture of the school and the culture of the home.

Good teachers working in intergenerational programs have used their own forms of alternative knowledge and their own experiences to generate new knowledge. One teacher in a program for immigrant parents and children in a rural, economically depressed area along the Rio Grande River in Texas developed a lesson on Halloween in the United States. He not only provided homemade costume ideas, materials, and assistance in the making of the costumes, but he also compared the origins and cultural traditions of the U.S. holiday with the Day of the Dead holiday traditions in Mexico and Central America (Quintero & Macías, in press).

Risk: Generative Self-Confidence

Risk can also be a positive force in intergenerational literacy programs, because it can generate self-confidence. One positive instance of a parent's risk-taking in a family literacy project occurred when attention was given to the topic of parents advocating for their children. A lesson was developed on "School and You: Avenues for Advocacy," because several of the parents had inquired or expressed discontent and frustration with encounters in their children's schools. The class discussion focused on the different procedures that parents could use within the school systems to voice their complaints and advocate for change. One parent felt that her child's bilingual teacher was treating the child in a disrespectful way, damaging the child's self-confidence, and inhibiting her learning. Three months later this parent reported having discussed this situation with other parents who shared similar stories. They convened at the school to brainstorm how they could deal with "children's abuse by teachers." Apparently these parents recognized that psychological and cognitive abuse was taking place in their children's classrooms, and they were prepared to take collective action (Quintero & Macías, in press).

Lily Wong Fillmore (1991), a researcher in second-language learning and early education, has spearheaded a nationwide research project regarding the effects of early education efforts to teach very young children a second language. The preliminary findings of this study show that not only do most of these children lose their first language in the process, but there are very tragic losses in family communication. Cultural values and traditional childrearing principles are not communicated. Give and take conversations, which are the backbone of relationships, cease to exist. Fillmore (1991) contends that

teachers and parents must work together to try to mitigate the harm that can be done to children when they discover that differences are not welcome in the social world represented by the school. Parents need to be warned of the consequences of not insisting that their children speak to them in the language of the home. (p. 345)

An Ojibwa mother and university student in Minnesota speaks of risk and the resulting self-confidence that has changed her life and is providing new information for children in schools where she speaks and performs:

I am a Native American and a member from the Red Lake Indian Reservation. I'm proud of who I am and proud of what I stand for. I believe Indian people are very special people with a lot of special abilities. But there were times when being an Indian was painful. Sometimes I would wish that I could have washed off the color of my skin or changed my hair color because of all the racial remarks that I encountered. It hurt me as a person and my self-image, and self-esteem....It was difficult to go to school because I was an Indian. I think all I did was fight....Now I'm using other means to fight with. Instead of physical violence, I use methods, such as my mind. Instead of letting the anger control me and my actions, I use the anger. With educational methods. I find ways to educate non-Indians, by going to my daughter's classroom and explaining about our culture. My family and I dance at schools to show the non-Indian student what the meaning of dances are about. I make myself visible instead of invisible.

(Education student, University of Minnesota, Duluth)

Children are willing to share their own reality when they perceive that it will be respected and valued. A child in one family literacy program did not hesitate to comment during a music lesson that her favorite musical group was *Los Buquis*, a group unknown in Anglo societies, and even in assimilated Hispanic societies. In another class, during a lesson on plants, the instructor asked, *"¿Para que sirven los arboles?"* (How are trees useful?). One child raised his hand and answered, *"Para secar la ropa"* (To dry our clothes), and another answered *"Para darle sombra al carro"* (To provide shade for the car). In a different lesson on emotions the instructor asked, *"¿Cuándo te sientes así?"* (When do you feel like this?), as he pointed to a drawing of a happy face. The child answered, *"Cuando me dejan ir al río"* (When they let me go to the river). Another student responded, *"Cuando me compran hamburguesas"* (When they buy me hamburgers). Mexicans do not eat only tacos.

Another child, four years old, did not hesitate to risk his perception of reality in the following drawing:

The teacher remarked, *"¡Que bonito! Dime de tu dibujo"* (How pretty! Tell me about your drawing). Ivan responded, *"Se está llendo al cielo. Mi mamá dice que todos nosotros vamos a ir al cielo"* (He's going up to heaven. My mother says that we are all going to go up to heaven).

Another child, five years old, risked the teacher's reprimand in a class. The theme of the class was community helpers. The teacher opened the lesson by asking questions about community helpers and was clearly guiding the children to talk about traditional helpers, such as firefighters, doctors, and bakers.

T: "What would you like to be, Victor?"

V: *"A Ghostbuster, a cuidar mi hermano."* (A Ghostbuster, so I can take care of my brother.)

T: "Is a Ghostbuster a community helper? No. What about a fireman, a policeman, or something like that?

Both Piagetian and Vygotskyan researchers have taught us that child cognition is nurtured by imagination and meaningful social relationships. Cazden (1981), Cummins (1989), González-Mena (1981), Goodman (1986), and others have pointed out that young children learn a second language through rich, interactive language environments. Teacher education scholars tell us that "teaching against the grain" (Cochran-Smith, 1991) is not only more effective, but also the most ethical approach for students in a pluralistic world. This teacher missed an opportunity to build on Victor's creative thinking about community helpers and his desire to care for his brother.

Cochran-Smith (1991) urges teachers to have the self-confidence to take risks in order to teach against the grain, and teachers participating in family literacy projects have taken risks do this. One teacher commented in her journal:

With the teaching experiences I've had, I have to say my teaching is changing. Not drastically, but it is evident. I can recall doing my student teaching. Despite my survival (after completing over 400 hours) my teaching esteem was not very high. True, I gained from observing other teachers at work, but their styles did not affect or inspire me. Now after a few teaching jobs I have witnessed growth within myself. This growth has been affected by the children. Because of them, I've pushed myself to provide interesting activities that are appropriate. My confidence increases with each opportunity. This family literacy project has provided me with unforgettable experiences. Working with parents has also added to my growth. I know with every experience comes change, and luckily mine have been positive. With change though, I always keep in mind to respect my students. For it is through respect that I will gain as well. Moreover, I accept and acknowledge them, because without them, growth would not result.

Fillmore (1990), in the course of her research about what is wrong with second language early education, also gives us hope through her identification of some risk-taking teachers working with Latino families. She explained that these teachers are "mostly women from the same background as the parents of the children in the center" (p. 33) and described the strong staff development component of the program. She concluded,

> The teachers are cultural and linguistic bridges connecting the worlds of the home and the classroom; they facilitate the children's entry to school by building on what the children have learned in their homes. The family is drawn into the life and work of the Center rather than dismissed as irrelevant. (pp. 33-34)

Finally, for those of us who are willing to take the risks—to cross academic and funding lines and form links between child and adult programs, schools and community agencies, elders and children, practitioners and researchers, always relying on our participants' strengths and our own creative ability and tenacity—perhaps we will become a type of educational "mixed blood": the "catch," as Dorris and Erdrich's (1991) character, Vivian, describes herself:

> I belong to the lost tribe of mixed bloods, that hodgepodge amalgam of hue and cry that defies easy placement. When the DNA of my various ancestors—Irish and Coeur d'Alene and Spanish and Navajo and God knows what else—combined to form me, the result was not some genteel, undecipherable puree that comes from a Cuisinart. You know what they say on the side of the Bisquick box, under instructions for pancakes? Mix with a fork. Leave lumps. That was me....We're called marginal, as if we exist anywhere but on the center of the page. Our territory is the place for asides, for explanatory notes, for editorial notation. But there are advantages to peripheral vision....We have our roles to play. "Caught between two worlds" is the way it's often characterized, but I'd put it differently. We are the catch. (pp. 123-124)

By crossing many of the barriers regarding acceptable knowledge and alternative ways of knowing, and barriers of the generations, educators learn to include and value the cultural diversity of their students, and, in turn, the students learn to value the educational experience of the classroom.

References

Bloch, M.N. (1991). Critical science and the history of child development's influence on early education research. *Early Education and Development, 2*(2), 95-108.

Cazden, C. (1981). *Language in early childhood education.* Washington, DC: National Association for the Education of Young Children.

Cochran-Smith, M. (1991). Learning to teach against the grain. *Harvard Education Review, 61*(3), 279-310.

Coles, R. (1990). *The spiritual life of children.* Boston: Houghton Mifflin.

Cummins, J. (1989). *Empowering minority students.* Sacramento, CA: California Association for Bilingual Education.

Dorris, M., & Erdrich, L. (1991). *The crown of Columbus.* New York: Harper Collins.

Edelsky, C. (1990). Whose agenda is this anyway? A response to McKenna, Robinson, and Miller. *Educational Researcher, 19*(8),7-11.

Fillmore, L.W. (1990). Latino families and the schools. In *California perspectives: An anthology* (pp. 30-37). Los Angeles: The Immigrant Writers Project. (ERIC Document Reproduction Service No. ED 349 134)

Fillmore, L.W. (1991). When learning a second language means losing the first. *Early Childhood Research Quarterly, 6*(3), 323-347.

González-Mena, J. (1981). English as a second language for preschool children. In C. Cazden (Ed.) *Language in early childhood education* (pp. 127-140). Washington, DC: National Association for the Education of Young Children.

Goodman, K. (1986). *What's whole in whole language.* Portsmouth, NH: Heinemann.

Kingston, M.H. (1977). *Woman warrior.* New York: Vintage.

Oakes, J., & Lipton, M. (1990). *Making the best of schools.* New Haven, CT: Yale University Press.

Quintero, E., & Macías, A.H. (in press). To participate, to speak out: A story from San Elizario, Texas. In R. Martin (Ed.), *On equal terms: Addressing issues of race, class and gender in higher education*. New York: State University of New York.

Stuecher, U. (1991). *Positive Indian parenting: A reference manual in support of Minnesota Indian parents and families*. St. Paul, MN: Minnesota Department of Education.

Weinstein-Shr, G. (1994). Literacy and second language learners: A family agenda. In D. Spener (Ed.), *Adult biliteracy in the United States* (pp. 111-122). Washington, DC and McHenry, IL: Center for Applied Linguistics and Delta Systems.

BIOGRAPHIES

Maritza Arrastía

Maritza Arrastía developed the community literature approach to literacy in collaboration with the teachers and students of the Mothers' Reading Program in New York City, where she worked as teacher/director from 1984 to 1992. She currently works with culture-based education methodologies—such as community literature, storytelling, and participatory dramas—as a literacy staff developer for New York City's Community Development Agency. She writes poetry, drama, and fiction and has published a novel, *Exile* (Atabex, 1991).

Elsa Auerbach

Elsa Auerbach teaches in the Bilingual/ESL Graduate Studies Program at the University of Massachusetts at Boston. She has taught ESL to adults in community and union programs and has coordinated several university-community collaborations, including family literacy and bilingual community literacy training projects. She is the author of *Making Meaning, Making Change: Participatory Curriculum Development for Adult ESL Literacy* (Center for Applied Linguistics and Delta Systems, 1992).

Jessica Dilworth

Jessica Dilworth is an adult educator with Pima County Adult Education in Tucson, Arizona. She teaches classes and trains teachers in family literacy, ESOL, GED, computers, family math and science, and group dynamics. As ESOL Curriculum Coordinator, she wrote a learner-directed, participatory ESOL curriculum for adult education.

Dan Doorn

Dan Doorn, Associate Professor in Education at Azusa Pacific University, specializes in the process of children's language and literacy development across the curriculum. His explorations of ways to enrich and integrate learning for bilingual children have included classroom-based research in Hispanic and Native American schools in New Mexico and in Micronesian schools in the Pacific. His most valued teaching insights continue to come from observing children making personal discoveries together in a caring community of learners.

Daniel D. Holt

Daniel D. Holt has worked as a consultant in the Bilingual Education Office, California Department of Education, since 1977. He has edited a number of publications on the evaluation of family English literacy programs, bilingual education, and cooperative learning. Before joining the department, he was a volunteer and staff member with the Peace Corps in Korea from 1970 to 1976.

Grace D. Holt

Grace D. Holt is the coordinator of the Family English Literacy Program in the Sacramento City Unified School District. She is also a consultant in adult literacy and an author of numerous adult ESL materials, including *Parenting Curriculum for Language Minority Parents* (1988). From 1986 to 1989, she was the coordinator of the Family English Literacy Program at California State University, Sacramento. Her work with nonnative English speaking adults began in 1972, when she was a volunteer with the Peace Corps in Korea.

Ana Huerta-Macías

Ana Huerta-Macías is an assistant professor in curriculum and instruction at New Mexico State University. Her teaching and research interests have led her in the past 15 years to work and publish in the areas of teacher development, ESL, bilingualism, bilingual education, and most recently, parent involvement and family literacy. She was previously Co-Director of Project FIEL in El Paso, Texas.

Nora Lewis

Nora Lewis was recruited as one of the first volunteer tutors in Philadelphia's Project LEIF, and eventually she served as both learning center coordinator and project director for the program. She is currently Coordinator for Business Programs at the English Language Programs of the University of Pennsylvania and a doctoral candidate in educational linguistics. Her research interests lie in the areas of second language acquisition, adult literacy, and English for specific purposes program and curriculum design.

Loren McGrail

Loren McGrail is the literacy specialist for the Massachusetts System for Adult Basic Education Support (SABES) at World Education in Boston. Her current focus and work include participatory approaches in adult ESOL, learner-centered approaches to assessment, family literacy, and teachers-as-researchers. She is a contributing author to *Talking Shop: A Curriculum Sourcebook for Participatory Adult ESL* (Center for Applied Linguistics and Delta Systems, 1992).

Elizabeth Quintero

Elizabeth Quintero is an assistant professor in education at the University of Minnesota in Duluth. Her educational background, teaching experience, research interests, and publications combine early childhood education with bilingual education. Her dissertation research on biliteracy development of Spanish-speaking preschoolers in a Head Start program and her interests in family contexts led to the design and implementation of Project FIEL in El Paso, Texas.

Brian V. Street

Brian Street is Senior Lecturer in Social Anthropology at the University of Sussux and Visiting Professor of Education in the Graduate School of Education, University of Pennsylvania. He undertook anthropological fieldwork in Iran during the 1970s and has since worked in the United States, Britain, and South Africa., He has written and lectured extensively on literacy practices and is best known for *Literacy in Theory and Practice* (1985). He recently edtied *Cross-Cultural Approaches to Literacy* (1993).

Cecelia Varbero

Cecelia Varbero is currently an instructor at Drexel University's English Language Center and an adjunct faculty member in humanities and communication. Her interests include all aspects of the writing process and issues of adjustment for immigrant and refugee families in the United States.

Gail Weinstein-Shr

Gail Weinstein-Shr established Temple University's Project LEIF, Learning English through Intergenerational Friendship, among Philadelphia's Southeast Asian refugee and Latino immigrant communities. It was this work that inspired her to give attention to the role of language and literacy in the relationships of grandparents, parents, and children. She is now on the faculty of San Francisco State University, where she specializes in preparing TESOL teacher trainees for work with adult immigrants and refugees. Her publications on adult ESL, literacy, and family issues include *Stories to Tell our Children*—an ESL collection for adults who are new users of English—as well as a guest-edited issue of *TESOL Quarterly* on the theme of adult literacies (Autumn 1993).

Heide Spruck Wrigley

Heide Spruck Wrigley works with the Southport Institute for Policy Analysis, where she directs a national study on policy issues in adult ESL. She is the outside evaluator for several workplace literacy and family literacy programs and specializes in issues related to evaluation, assessment, and accountability. A former ESL student herself, Wrigley now holds a Ph.D. in education with a specialization in language, literacy, and learning.

Language in Education: Theory and Practice

The Educational Resources Information Center (ERIC), which is supported by the Office of Educational Research and Improvement of the U.S. Department of Education, is a nationwide system of information centers, each responsible for a given educational level or field of study. ERIC's basic objective is to make developments in educational research, instruction, and teacher training readily accessible to educators and members of related professions.

The ERIC Clearinghouse on Languages and Linguistics (ERIC/CLL), one of the specialized information centers in the ERIC system, is operated by the Center for Applied Linguistics (CAL) and is specifically responsible for the collection and dissemination of information on research in languages and linguistics and on the application of research to language teaching and learning.

In 1989, CAL was awarded a contract to expand the activities of ERIC/CLL through the establishment of an adjunct ERIC clearinghouse, the National Clearinghouse for ESL Literacy Education (NCLE). NCLE's specific focus is literacy education for language minority adults and out-of-school youth.

ERIC/CLL and NCLE commission recognized authorities in languages, linguistics, adult literacy education, and English as a second language (ESL) to write about current issues in these fields. Monographs, intended for educators, researchers, and others interested in language education, are published under the series title, Language in Education: Theory and Practice (LIE). The *LIE* series includes practical guides for teachers, state-of-the-art papers, research reviews, and collected reports.

For further information on the ERIC system, ERIC/CLL, or NCLE, contact either clearinghouse at the Center for Applied Linguistics, 1118 22nd Street, NW, Washington, DC 20037.

Joy Kreeft Peyton, Fran Keenan, Series Editors
Vickie Lewelling, ERIC/CLL Publications Coordinator
Miriam J. Burt, NCLE Publications Coordinator

Other *LIE* Titles Available from Delta Systems

The following are other titles in the *Language in Education* series published by the Center for Applied Linguistics and Delta Systems Co., Inc.:

Adult Biliteracy in the United States (ISBN 0-937354-83-X)
edited by David Spener

Approaches to Adult ESL Literacy Instruction (ISBN 0-937354-82-1)
edited by JoAnn Crandall and Joy Kreeft Peyton

Assessing Success in Family Literacy Projects: Alternative Approaches to Assessment and Evaluation (ISBN 0-93-7354-85-6)
edited by Daniel D. Holt

Cooperative Learning: A Response to Linguistic and Cultural Diversity (ISBN 0-937354-81-3)
edited by Daniel D. Holt

Making Meaning, Making Change: Participatory Curriculum Development for Adult ESL Literacy (ISBN 0-937354-79-1)
by Elsa Roberts Auerbach

Speaking of Language: An International Guide to Language Service Organizations (ISBN 0-937354-80-5)
edited by Paula Conru, Vickie Lewelling, and Whitney Stewart

Talking Shop: A Curriculum Sourcebook for Participatory Adult ESL (ISBN 0-937354-78-3)
by Andrea Nash, Ann Cason, Madeline Rhum, Loren McGrail, and Rosario Gomez-Sanford

To order any of these titles, call Delta Systems, Co., Inc. at (800) 323-8270 or (815) 363-3582 (9-5 EST) or write to them at 1400 Miller Pkwy., McHenry, IL 60050.